MIS CASES: DECISION MAKING WITH APPLICATION SOFTWARE

MIS CASES: DECISION MAKING WITH APPLICATION SOFTWARE

M. Lisa Miller
University of Central Oklahoma

Pearson
Education

Upper Saddle River, New Jersey 07458

Acquisitions editor: Bob Horan
Project Manager: Kyle Hannon
Executive editor: David Alexander
Production editor: Carol Zaino
Manufacturer: VonHoffman Graphics/MO

ISBN 0-13-034832-5

10 9 8 7 6 5 4 3 2

Dedication

To my parents, James and Joan. Your encouragement, support, and understanding are a constant source of strength. You are truly the wind beneath my wings.

In memory of my grandmother, Mary. You touched the lives of your family and friends in such a strong, positive way. Your belief in education and the opportunities it brings is a lesson that your children, grandchildren, and great-grandchildren have taken to heart.

Table of Contents

Part III: Web Page Development

Preface

Introduction

MIS Cases: Decision Making with Application Software serves as a supplementary textbook for any business course where students are encouraged to use application software to solve managerial problems. *MIS Cases: Decision Making with Application Software* is especially useful for introductory management information systems, personal productivity, end user systems, and graduate, foundation-level management information systems courses. This casebook provides students with different case scenarios, emphasizes different software packages and their integration, emphasizes managerial problem solving, and provides varying levels of difficulty. By providing a variety of cases with different difficulty levels, the instructor can use this casebook as a leveling or teaching tool.

MIS Cases: Decision Making with Application Software contains numerous cases, reflecting human resource, production, accounting, financial, and marketing managerial decision-making situations. The cases present the student with managerial decision-making activities, ranging from basic problem-solving situations to more advanced problem-solving situations. The number and variety of cases enable the instructor to select the most appropriate cases for his class, as well as vary the cases between semesters.

This casebook contains nine database, nine spreadsheet and two Web page development cases. Several of the cases are integration cases. The integration cases require the students to apply their knowledge of more than one software package to solve a managerial problem. To prepare each case, the student will use spreadsheet, database, or Web page development software. Each case encourages the student to use his knowledge, creativity, and software skills to solve a realistic managerial problem.

Organization

MIS Cases: Decision Making with Application Software uses a standard format for each case. Each case has a difficulty rating, skills check, case background, case scenario, information specification, implementation concerns, test your design, and case deliverable sections. To facilitate the preparation of the database cases, the database case format also includes storage specification and input specification sections. Likewise, the spreadsheet and Web page development cases have a design specification section.

Each case is given a difficulty rating. The difficulty rating is intended to help the instructor determine the appropriateness of the case for his students. At the beginning of the case, one or more stars designate the difficulty rating. Cases with a one star rating are the easiest cases in the casebook, while cases with a five star rating are the more rigorous cases.

The skills check feature provides both the instructor and students with a list of the primary skills required to complete the case. The instructor may use the skills check list to determine the appropriateness of the case for his students and whether the case should be used as a leveling or a teaching tool. Students can use the skills check list to determine whether they need further study before attempting the case.

The case background section provides the instructor and student with a quick summary of the case. Again, this enables the instructor to determine the appropriateness of the case for his students. The case scenario section sets the stage for the application and decision-making activities, provides insights into how the case's main character will use the application and briefly identifies several of the case character's information requirements. The information specification section outlines additional information requirements for the case. The implementation concerns section provides final comments about the design and development of the application. This section also points out areas that may cause the student some concern and provides helpful hints about which tools or techniques the student can use to avoid potential trouble spots.

Once a student has developed the application, the test your design section requires the student to make modifications to his application. This section encourages the student to develop a flexible application that is adaptable to a manager's changing information needs. For instance, this section may require the student to generate a new query, add new records to a database, insert additional columns and formulas into a spreadsheet, or add additional content to a Web page.

The case deliverables section specifies what deliverables are to be submitted to the instructor. Each case requires the student to prepare both written and oral presentations for his case solution. This section also requires the student to provide working, electronic copies of his solution, hard copies, and results for the information requested by the case's character. The instructor, at his discretion, may require the student to submit one or all of the deliverables.

Support Material

An instructor's manual, student data files, and Web site are the primary support materials for this casebook. The instructor's manual contains teaching tips, additional comments about the cases, correlation guides, and suggested case solutions. The Web site provides online access to the instructor and student resources and contains updated cases and additional materials. The Web site is located at www.prenhall.com/miller.

Acknowledgements

As is true in most business settings, the accomplishment of a goal is a team effort. This casebook would not have been possible without the dedication and numerous contributions from my Prentice Hall team, students, colleagues, and family.

Robert Horan, Kyle Hannon, Jeanne Bronson, and Tabitha McCuan were instrumental in getting this project off the ground. I would especially like to thank Robert Horan and Kyle Hannon. Robert's wealth of knowledge, motivational emails, encouragement, and dedication to this project were obvious. Kyle's professionalism, guidance, support, and attention to detail definitely enhanced the quality of this casebook.

My University of Central Oklahoma students and colleagues provided many valuable comments and suggestions. I would like to thank Patricia Killman, Debbie Barnheiser-Alston, Sandy Smith, Margie Miano, and Gloria O'Dell for their helpful comments, ideas, and student perspectives. I would like to acknowledge the contributions of Dr. Saba Bahouth, Dr. Hassan Pourbabaee, Dr. Randall Ice, Dr. Robert Terrell, Dr. Bambi Hora, and Dr. Katherene Terrell. My sincerest appreciation goes to Dr. Hora. Dr. Hora was always willing to go the extra mile to help a colleague and a friend. Words cannot begin to express my deepest gratitude to Dr. Katherene Terrell for her encouragement from the beginning of this project to its end. Dr. Katherene Terrell has traveled this road several times and served as my mentor on this project. Her guidance, suggestions, wisdom, and advice on cases were greatly appreciated.

My family has been a tremendous support system during the preparation of this casebook. I cannot begin to thank the most important people in my life for their willingness to take a back seat while this casebook was being written. James, Joan, Tracy, Jacob, Danette, Baylee, and Caedee are my greatest inspirations. Finally, I must thank Greg for his support and encouragement.

CASE 1

Milligan's Backyard Storage Kits

Spreadsheet Case   **Difficulty Rating:** ★

CASE BACKGROUND

Milligan's Backyard Storage Kits, a mail order company, sells a variety of backyard storage unit kits and landscaping decorations to its customers. Although the company makes a profit, David Milligan, the company's owner, realizes that he can improve his company's operations if he better manages his inventory. Mr. Milligan requests your help in preparing an Inventory Analysis worksheet. The Inventory Analysis worksheet provides Mr. Milligan with information about his annual sales, cost of goods sold, gross profit, and markup on his products. Preparing the worksheet for Mr. Milligan requires you to insert columns, use several functions, and apply proper formatting to the worksheet and cells.

CASE SCENARIO

Ten years ago, David Milligan was short on storage space. After shopping around for a backyard storage unit and not finding one that met his specifications, Mr. Milligan built his own storage unit for his backyard. Realizing that many homeowners had similar storage needs, Mr. Milligan began selling a backyard storage unit kit via mail order. He felt that given good instructions, precut lumber, and the necessary hardware, just about anyone could assemble a storage unit. His idea proved popular, and he now stocks and sells 27 different items, including storage barn, gazebo, and landscaping decoration kits.

Mr. Milligan does not use a formal, consistent inventory tracking system. Periodically, Mr. Milligan or his staff visually checks to see which kits are in stock. Although he does try to keep a certain level of each kit in stock, the lack of a formal inventory tracking system has led to the overstocking of some items and understocking of still other items. In fact, on occasion, a customer will request a particular kit, and it is only then that Mr. Milligan realizes that the kit is out of stock. If a kit is not available, Mr. Milligan must tell the customer that he is currently out of stock, and then hope that the customer will wait for a kit to become available.

Lately, Mr. Milligan has become concerned with his inventory management methods. He now wants to better manage his inventory. As a starting point, he wants to examine his costs, sales, markup percentages, gross profits, and inventory levels. He asks you to review his inventory and make suggestions for improvement. He provides you with the data contained in Figure 1 and asks you to prepare an Inventory Analysis worksheet.

Figure 1: Inventory Data

Milligan's Backyard Storage Units
Inventory Data

Item No.	Description	Unit Cost	Unit Sales Price	Average On Hand	Average Unit Sales/Year
A00100	8' x 6' Aluminum Shed	$148.14	$199.99	50	500
A00110	10' x 8' Aluminum Shed	$185.17	$249.99	50	400
A00120	12' x 20' Aluminum Shed	$1,393.56	$1,950.99	50	75
A00130	6' x 4' Aluminum Shed	$346.36	$519.59	50	241
A00140	8' x 4' Aluminum Shed	$442.85	$620.75	50	215
A00210	8' x 10' Aluminum Barn	$840.47	$1,050.59	75	199
A00310	12' x 8' Double Door Aluminum Shed	$1,043.57	$1,304.47	80	302
A00320	16' x 10' Double Door Aluminum Shed	$1,141.84	$1,507.24	10	50
A00410	8' x 10' Wood Barn	$514.03	$804.49	50	700
A00420	8' x 12' Wood Barn	$751.87	$999.99	50	140
A00430	10' x 16' Wood Barn	$808.26	$1,074.99	10	75
A00510	8' x 10' Picnic Table	$296.28	$399.99	25	325
A00520	3' by 7' Picnic Table	$199.93	$299.99	75	900
A00610	10' Octagon Cedar Gazebo	$2,399.99	$2,999.99	75	150
A00710	4' x 6' Cedar Shed	$333.33	$500.00	80	200
A00720	8' x 10' Cedar Shed	$1,135.32	$1,702.99	80	75
A00730	6' x 10' Cedar Garden Hut	$1,135.00	$1,350.00	80	175
A00740	8' x 10' Cedar Cabana Shed	$1,148.56	$1,607.99	75	136
A00750	6' x 6' Cedar Garden Hut	$879.99	$950.78	125	402
A00620	12' Cedar Octagon Gazebo	$2,963.99	$3,430.99	15	43
A00810	6' x 20' Covered Bridge	$1,200.00	$1,400.99	42	75
A00910	Wagon Planter	$10.66	$15.99	250	900
A00920	Mailbox Planter	$18.66	$27.99	250	845
A00930	4' Windmill	$30.66	$45.99	275	201
A00940	6' Windmill	$43.99	$65.99	300	278

| A00950 | 6' Wishing Well | $53.32 | $79.99 | 300 | 780 |
| A00960 | 12' Wishing Well | $130.66 | $195.99 | 25 | 147 |

Design Specifications

Mr. Milligan asks you to determine the cost of average inventory, annual sales, cost of goods sold, annual gross profit, gross margin ratio, and markup percentage for each inventory item. The determination of these values requires you to add columns to the Inventory Analysis worksheet. Mr. Milligan asks you to use the formulas shown in Figure 2.

Since Mr. Milligan will use the Inventory Analysis worksheet during a presentation, he wants the worksheet to have a professional appearance. To enhance the worksheet's appearance, you include an appropriate header and format the worksheet, column, and row labels. The header should display the name of the business, the name of the worksheet, and the current date. As you construct the worksheet, you use the currency format for all columns containing dollar values. Also, for any column that contains a percentage, you use the percentage format and format the data to two decimal places.

Figure 2: Inventory Analysis Worksheet Formulas

Inventory Analysis Worksheet Formulas	
Annual Gross Profit	Annual Sales - Cost of Goods Sold
Annual Sales	Unit Sales Price * Average Unit Sales Per Year
Cost of Average Inventory	Unit Cost * Average Units On Hand
Cost of Goods Sold	Unit Cost * Average Unit Sales Per Year
Gross Margin Ratio	$\dfrac{\text{Gross Profit}}{\text{Annual Sales Per Unit}}$
Markup Based on Cost	$\dfrac{\text{Unit Sales Price - Unit Cost}}{\text{Unit Cost}}$

Information Specifications

For the cost of average inventory, annual sales, cost of goods sold, annual gross profit, gross margin ratio, and markup percentage values, Mr. Milligan wants the average, minimum and maximum value for each. Mr. Milligan wants to know the maximum unit cost and sales price, as well as the minimum unit cost and sales price. He also wants to know the total cost of average inventory, total annual gross profit, total cost of goods sold, and the total annual sales.

Mr. Milligan also needs answers to the following questions. Using your newly designed Inventory Analysis worksheet, provide Mr. Milligan with answers to his questions.

1. Mr. Milligan wants a markup of at least 25 percent on all items. Which items have markups less than 25 percent?

2. In terms of dollars, which item has the lowest sales?

3. In terms of dollars, what were Mr. Milligan's biggest selling items last year? Identify the top five.

4. What are the company's total annual sales?

5. What is the company's annual gross profit?

Implementation Concerns

While you are free to work with the design of your worksheet, the worksheet should have a consistent, professional appearance. Also, you should use appropriate formatting for the cells and worksheet. For instance, dollar values should display a dollar sign and be formatted to two decimal places.

Test Your Design

After creating the Inventory Analysis worksheet, you should test your design. Perform the following steps. Keep in mind that you may need to insert additional columns to provide Mr. Milligan with this information.

1. For each inventory item, Mr. Milligan wants to know what percentage of the company's total annual sales the item generated.

2. What is the gross margin per unit for each inventory item? Which inventory item(s) has the largest gross margin per unit? Least?

3. Mr. Milligan wants to reduce his inventory by $100,000. Which items would you recommend that he remove from his inventory? Why?

CASE DELIVERABLES

In order to satisfactorily complete this case, you should build the worksheet as described in the case scenario and then prepare both written and oral presentations. Unless otherwise specified, submit the following deliverables to your professor. Also, unless otherwise specified, perform these steps after you have tested your design.

1. A written report discussing any assumptions you have made about the case and the key elements of the case. Additionally, what features did you add to make the worksheet more functional? User friendly? (Please note that these assumptions cannot violate any of the requirements specified above and must be approved by your professor.)

2. A printout of the worksheet.

3. A printout of the worksheet's formulas.

4. An electronic, working copy of your worksheet that meets the criteria mentioned in the case scenario and specifications sections.

5. Results for each question posed above. (A memo to your instructor discussing these results should also be provided.)

6. As mentioned above, you should prepare an oral presentation. (Your instructor will establish the time allocated to your presentation.) You should use a presentation package and discuss the key features of your worksheet. Also, discuss how the worksheet is beneficial for Mr. Milligan. What additional information should be included in the worksheet to make it more useful?

CASE

2

Piedmont Trailer
Manufacturing Company

Spreadsheet Case   **Difficulty Rating:** ★

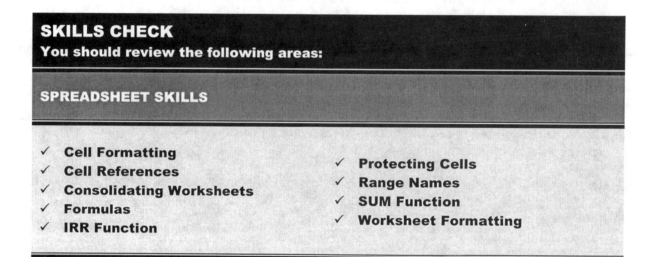

SKILLS CHECK

You should review the following areas:

SPREADSHEET SKILLS

- ✓ Cell Formatting
- ✓ Cell References
- ✓ Consolidating Worksheets
- ✓ Formulas
- ✓ IRR Function

- ✓ Protecting Cells
- ✓ Range Names
- ✓ SUM Function
- ✓ Worksheet Formatting

CASE BACKGROUND

Piedmont Trailer Manufacturing Company, a nationally recognized trailer manufacturer, produces a wide range of quality standard and custom-built trailers, ranging from gooseneck to bumper pull trailers. Although the Piedmont Trailer Manufacturing Company uses state of the art information systems for most of its business processes, its custom order tracking process is primarily manual-based and requires major renovations. In an effort to improve the custom order tracking process, a systems analysis and design project is currently underway. As part of the systems development team, one of your responsibilities is to prepare an economic feasibility analysis for an upcoming presentation to management.

Ms. Geraldine Pablo, the project manager, asks you to construct an Economic Feasibility workbook. The purpose of this workbook is to summarize and analyze the benefits and costs associated with the proposed custom order tracking project. The preparation of an Economic Feasibility workbook requires you to design five worksheets, use several formulas and functions, use basic cell and worksheet formatting, and consolidate data from multiple worksheets into a summary worksheet.

CASE SCENARIO

Quality trailers and excellent customer service are the two primary reasons why the Piedmont Trailer Manufacturing Company is the nation's largest manufacturer of standard and custom-built trailers. Although the majority of the company's income is derived from the sale of standard trailers, the number of custom orders is on the rise. When a custom order is placed, the request is captured on several paper forms and then routed to the production department. Often it takes three months before a custom order is released to production. This is due in part to the careful attention given to the customer by helping him select the right finishes, fixtures, trailer size, and other amenities. Management has decided that the custom ordering process is inefficient, time consuming, and costly. In an effort to improve the custom order tracking process, your project team is assigned the task of developing a custom order tracking system.

During the planning phase, your project team identified several tangible benefits and costs. The new custom order tracking system will save the company money by decreasing storage, staff, and order rework expenses. Additionally, the proposed system should increase sales, improve order processing speed, and provide better data management. Table 1 summarizes these benefits and their respective savings.

The proposed custom order tracking system will incur both one-time and recurring costs. From one of your business courses, you recall that one-time costs often occur during the start up and development of a project, and recurring costs occur throughout the useful life of the new system. The one-time costs for this project currently include development personnel, training, project-related technology purchases, site-preparation, and miscellaneous costs. Table 2 lists the one-time costs and their estimated dollar values. Recurring costs include software maintenance, hardware, supplies, a new information technology position, and site rental costs. Table 3 summarizes these recurring costs.

Table 1: Yearly Recurring Benefits

Benefit	Approximate Dollar Value
Storage Savings	$15,000
Staff Reduction (2 people)	$45,000
Reduced Order Rework	$10,000
Increased Sales	$75,000
Faster Order Processing	$25,000
Better Data Management	$125,000

Table 2: One-Time Costs

One-Time Cost	Approximate Dollar Value
Development Personnel	$100,000
Training	$45,000
Project-Related Technology Purchases	$42,000
Site Preparation	$58,500
Miscellaneous	
Conference-Related	$6,000
Supplies	$1,908
Duplication	$3,249

Table 3: Yearly Recurring Costs

Cost	Approximate Dollar Value
Software Maintenance	$50,000
Hardware	$45,000
Supplies	$25,000
IT Positions (1person)	$58,000
Site Rental	$24,000

Design Specifications

Since the project is in the early stages of development, you want your workbook to be as flexible as possible, so that additional costs and benefits, when identified, are easily added to the Economic Feasibility workbook. You decide that the Economic Feasibility workbook should contain at least five worksheets: Documentation, One-Time Cost, Recurring Cost, Tangible Benefit, and Economic Feasibility Summary. The Documentation worksheet provides information about the creator, each individual worksheet, and the date created. (Your professor will provide additional guidelines for the Documentation worksheet.)

You decide to construct the One-Time Cost, Recurring Cost, and Tangible Benefit worksheets first, since these worksheets have a simple design. These worksheets each contain two columns, with the first column identifying the items in the category, and the second column containing the dollar values associated with the items. Each worksheet totals the dollar values; these totals are then used in the Economic Feasibility Summary worksheet.

As Figure 1 shows, the Economic Feasibility Summary worksheet has a more complex design. Since the Economic Feasibility Summary worksheet is a summary worksheet, it consolidates data from the One-Time Cost, Recurring Cost, and Tangible Benefit worksheets, requiring you to reference specific cells on these worksheets.

CASE 2: Piedmont Trailer Manufacturing Company

As part of the Economic Feasibility Summary worksheet design, you must discount the recurring benefits and costs to their present values. Although several ways exist to determine the present value of the benefits, you decide to multiply the recurring benefit (or cost) by a present value factor. Since each year requires a different present value factor, the worksheet must compute the present value factor for each year. You decide to use the formula provided below to determine each year's present value factor. (In the following formula, "i" refers to the discount rate, and "n" refers to the year. The worksheet shown in Figure 1 assumes that the project's useful life is five years.) To determine the present value of a benefit or cost for a particular year, you multiply the recurring value of the benefit or cost for that year by the present value factor for that year. The net present value of all benefits (or costs) is a summation of the benefits (or costs) up to and including the current year. The overall net present value is the difference between the net present value of all benefits and the net present value of all costs. The cash flow section provides a summary of the cash flows on a yearly basis, as well as a summation of the overall cash flows.

$$PVF = 1/(1+i)^n$$

Figure 1: Economic Feasibility Summary Worksheet*

Piedmont Trailer Manufacturing Company Custom Order Tracking Project (Current Date)							
Discount Rate	.14						
				Year			
	0	1	2	3	4	5	Totals
Benefits							
Recurring Value of Benefits	$0.00	$295,000.00	$295,000.00	$295,000.00	$295,000.00	$295,000.00	
Present Value Factor	1.0000	.877193	.769468	.674972	.592080	.519369	
Present Value of Benefits	$0.00	$258,771.93	$226,992.92	$199,116.60	$174,663.68	$153,213.76	
Net Present Value of All Benefits	$0.00	$258,771.93	$485,764.85	$684,881.45	$859,545.13	$1,012,758.89	$1,012,758.89
Costs							
One-Time Costs	$256,657.00						
Recurring Costs	$0.00	$202,000.00	$202,000.00	$202,000.00	$202,000.00	$202,000.00	
Present Value Factor	1.0000	.877193	.769468	.674972	.592080	.519369	
Present Value of the Recurring Costs	$0.00	$177,193.00	$155,432.00	$136,344.00	$119,600.00	$104,912.00	
Net Present Value of All Costs	$256,657.00	$433,849.98	$589,282.42	$725,626.67	$845,226.89	$950,139.36	$950,139.36
Overall Net Present Value							$62,619.53
Cash Flow Analysis							
Yearly NPV Cash Flow	($256,657.00)	$81,578.95	$71,560.48	$62,772.35	$55,063.47	$48,301.29	
Overall NPV Cash Flow	($256,657.00)	($175,078.05)	($103,517.57)	($40,745.22)	$14,318.24	$62,619.53	

*Adapted from Modern Systems Analysis and Design, third edition, Jeffrey A. Hoffer, Joey F. George, and Joseph S. Valacich

Although Ms. Pablo is the primary user of the Economic Feasibility workbook, other project team members will have access to this workbook. Therefore, you decide that all cells, other than input cells, should be protected. (You may wish to use your system's online help feature to review worksheet protection.)

Information Specifications

Ms. Pablo wants to generate optimistic, realistic, and pessimistic views of the data, so she requests the ability to quickly change the discount rate. To satisfy this requirement, you include a cell on your Economic Feasibility Summary worksheet to hold the discount rate. Figure 1 shows that the discount rate is placed at the top of the worksheet. The discount rate is used in several formulas, so referencing this cell in a formula facilitates the economic feasibility analysis.

The Economic Feasibility Summary worksheet summarizes the costs and benefits, shows the present values of the costs and benefits, calculates the overall net present value, and shows the yearly and overall cash flows for the project. Although not shown in Figure 1, Ms. Pablo requests that the project's breakeven point and internal rate of return be determined. During her presentation to management, Ms. Pablo will use the breakeven point to help justify the project's viability and show how quickly management will recover its investment in the project. Since the internal rate of return provides an indication of the project's profitability, Ms. Pablo will use the internal rate of return to help justify management's investment in the project.

Ms. Pablo needs answers to the following questions. Using your newly designed Economic Feasibility workbook, provide Ms. Pablo with answers to her questions.

1. How will discount rates of 10, 12, and 14 percent affect the project's feasibility?

2. If management stipulates that the internal rate of return must be equal to or greater than the discount rate, is this project still justifiable?

3. How will eliminating an additional staff position of $25,000 affect the economic feasibility assessment?

4. Assume that the staff position mentioned in Step 3 is eliminated and that the site preparation cost increases to $95,000. What impact will these changes have on the project's feasibility?

Implementation Concerns

To design the Economic Feasibility workbook described in the case scenario, you will create a workbook consisting of five worksheets. You should create separate worksheets for the documentation, one-time costs, recurring costs, recurring benefits, and economic feasibility summary. Since the Economic Feasibility Summary worksheet consolidates data from three of the worksheets, you should create this worksheet last. You should also consider using range names to simplify the consolidation process.

While you are free to work with the design of your worksheets, each worksheet should have a consistent, professional appearance. You should also use proper formatting for the cells. For instance, dollar values should display with a dollar sign and be formatted to two decimal places.

Test Your Design

After creating the Economic Feasibility workbook described in the case scenario, you should test the design of your worksheets. Perform the following operations.

1. What recommendations would you make if the useful life of the project is three years instead of five years? Six years?

2. Identify at least three additional benefits that might be derived from this project. Estimate their value and include the values in your analysis. What impact do these new benefits have on your economic feasibility?

3. Identify at least one additional one-time cost and at least three additional recurring costs. Estimate their values and include these values in your analysis. What impact do these new costs have on your economic feasibility? Is the project still justifiable? Why or why not?

CASE DELIVERABLES

In order to satisfactorily complete this case, you should build the workbook as described in the case scenario and then prepare both written and oral presentations. Unless otherwise specified, submit the following deliverables to your professor. Also, unless otherwise specified, perform these steps after you have tested your design.

1. A written report discussing any assumptions you have made about the case and the key elements of the case. Additionally, what features did you add to make the worksheets more functional? User friendly? (Please note that these assumptions cannot violate any of the requirements specified above and must be approved by your professor.)

2. A printout of each worksheet.

3. A printout of each worksheet's formulas.

4. An electronic, working copy of your workbook that meets the criteria mentioned in the case scenario and specifications sections.

5. Results for each question posed above. (A memo to your instructor discussing these results should also be provided.)

6. As mentioned above, you should prepare an oral presentation. (Your instructor will establish the time allocated to your presentation.) You should use a presentation package and discuss the key features of your worksheets. Also, discuss how the workbook is beneficial for Ms. Pablo. What additional information should be included in the workbook to make it more useful?

Maxi's Grocery Mart

Spreadsheet Case   **Difficulty Rating:** ★★

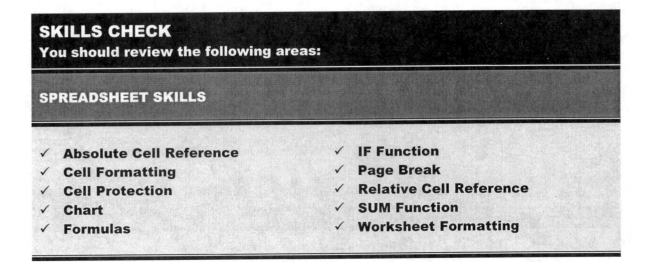

SKILLS CHECK
You should review the following areas:

SPREADSHEET SKILLS

- ✓ Absolute Cell Reference
- ✓ Cell Formatting
- ✓ Cell Protection
- ✓ Chart
- ✓ Formulas

- ✓ IF Function
- ✓ Page Break
- ✓ Relative Cell Reference
- ✓ SUM Function
- ✓ Worksheet Formatting

CASE BACKGROUND

Since its opening almost 50 years ago, Maxi's Grocery Mart has continued to grow and evolve with the times. The family-owned business has survived many ups and downs and is currently experiencing a modest growth in business. Leroy Feronti, the current owner, wants to expand his family's business by renovating the grocery mart building. While Mr. Feronti has some personal funds available, he will need to procure a loan from the local bank. Before approaching the local bank, he would like to prepare and review several pro forma financial statements. If Mr. Feronti decides to go forward with the renovation, he will use the pro forma financial statements as part of his loan application. Mr. Feronti wants the pro forma income statement prepared first, and he asks you to prepare it for him. Preparation of the pro forma income statement requires you to design a worksheet with input and information sections, properly format the worksheet, construct simple formulas, perform what if analysis, and generate a chart.

CASE SCENARIO

Maxi's Grocery Mart is a family-owned business that has been in operation since the 1950s. Although Leroy Feronti is very active with his business, he does employ a store manager, assistant manager, and 15 full-time employees. The manager and assistant manager are paid a salary, and the employees are paid an hourly wage. Each employee works 40 hours a week, 50 weeks a year.

Having recently assumed ownership of the business from his parents, Mr. Feronti feels that one of the keys to the business's continued success is the renovation of the grocery mart building. Renovating the existing building will cost approximately $450,000. Mr. Feronti must borrow $300,000 from the local bank and will use income generated from the grocery mart to repay the loan. Mr. Feronti asks you to prepare a set of pro forma financial statements for him. He will use these statements to analyze his business. If he decides to pursue the renovation project, he will use the pro forma statements as part of his loan application.

Mr. Feronti asks you to use the income statement outline shown in Figure 1 and use the grocery mart's 2002 sales as the base period. You will use the 2002 sales to calculate Mr. Feronti's sales, cost of goods sold, expenses, taxes, and net income for the next three years. When preparing the pro forma income statement, several assumptions and additional information are necessary. Figure 2 provides these assumptions and additional information.

Figure 1: Maxi's Food Mart Income Statement Outline

Maxi's Food Mart Pro Forma Income Statement				
	2002	2003	2004	2005
Sales				
Deli	Assume 5 percent of total sales each year.			
Dairy	Assume 20 percent of total sales each year.			
Canned Goods	Assume 15.5 percent of total sales each year.			
Frozen Foods	Assume 18 percent of total sales each year.			
Meats	Assume 21 percent of total sales each year.			
Produce	Assume 12.5 percent of total sales each year.			
Dry Goods	Assume 8 percent of total sales each year.			
Total Sales	Assume $3,500,000.00 in total sales for 2002.			
Cost of Goods Sold				
Deli	Assume 50 percent of deli sales each year.			
Dairy	Assume 50 percent of dairy sales each year.			
Canned Goods	Assume 75 percent of canned good sales each year.			
Frozen Foods	Assume 65 percent of frozen food sales each year.			
Meats	Assume 50 percent of meat sales each year.			
Produce	Assume 75 percent of produce sales each year.			
Dry Goods	Assume 66 percent of dry good sales each year.			
Total Cost of Goods Sold				
Gross Profit				

Operating Expenses				
Sales and Marketing	Assume 5.5 percent of total sales each year.			
General and Administrative	Assume 8.75 percent of total sales each year.			
Depreciation	Assume $20,000 per year.			
Wages	Includes the employees' wages, manager's salary, and assistant manager's salary.			
Common Costs	Mr. Feronti's salary.			
Total Operating Expenses				
Income Before Taxes				
Income Taxes				
Net Income				

Figure 2: Assumptions and Additional Information

Maxi's Food Mart	
Assumptions and Additional Information	
Growth and Tax Rates	**Salary**
2003 Growth: 7.00 percent	Leroy: 15 percent of gross profit
2004 Growth: 7.50 percent	Manager: $50,000
2005 Growth: 8.00 percent	Assistant Manager: $36,000
Tax Rate: 35 percent	Employee Hourly Wage: $10.00

Design Specifications

Since Mr. Feronti will use the pro forma income statement as part of his loan application, he requests that it have a consistent, professional, and well-organized appearance. Mr. Feronti specifically requests that you include an appropriate header and apply proper formatting to the cells and worksheet.

Using Figures 1 and 2 as guides, you decide that the worksheet requires both input and information sections. Figure 2 provides the necessary data for the input section, and Figure 1 provides an outline and guidelines for constructing the information section. By creating separate sections, it is easy for Mr. Feronti to not only view the input data to his income statement, but also, if necessary, change the parameters, thus facilitating his decision-making activities.

The information section contains the pro forma income statement, and this section provides Mr. Feronti with information about his projected sales, cost of goods sold, operating expenses, and net income for years 2003 - 2005. The information section uses the grocery mart's 2002 sales as the basis for these projections. You make sure that, where appropriate, the information section formulas reference the cell values contained in the input section.

As you study Figure 1, you realize that Mr. Feronti wants his store item sales, cost of goods sold, and operating expenses expressed as a percentage of total sales. To facilitate Mr. Feronti's analysis, you place the total sales value in the input section, along with the other assumptions. By doing this, your formulas in the information section can reference the actual total sales figure. As you study Figure 2, you notice that Mr. Feronti's salary is 15 percent of the gross profit. Since Mr. Feronti only draws his salary if the grocery mart makes a profit, you must build this logic into the income statement. You do so by using the IF function. To keep the information section's formulas from accidentally being updated, you protect the cells in the information section.

Mr. Feronti wants the input and information sections printed on separate pages. However, he wants each section fitted on the page. The printouts should utilize a portrait orientation and be centered horizontally and vertically.

Information Specifications

Mr. Feronti needs information to support his decision making about the upcoming renovation to Maxi's Grocery Mart. Using the newly constructed pro forma income statement, provide Mr. Feronti with the information that he needs. (Before answering each of the following questions, reset your worksheet to its original values.)

1. What impact will sales growths of 9 percent in 2003, 9.5 percent in 2004, and 10 percent in 2005 have on the grocery mart's net income?

2. What impact will sales growths of 4 percent in 2003, 5 percent in 2004, and 5.5 in 2005 have on Mr. Feronti's net income?

3. Mr. Feronti wants a chart that compares the store items based on their 2002 sales. He asks you to select an appropriate chart type and then prepare the chart.

4. If Mr. Feronti decreases his salary to 8 percent and increases the employees' hourly wages to $11, what impact will this have on the grocery mart's net income?

5. Assume Mr. Feronti has 17 employees instead of 15. What impact will two additional employees have on the business's net income?

Implementation Concerns

The preparation of this case requires you to apply basic spreadsheet construction concepts. Since Mr. Feronti will change the input values during his decision-making activities, you should have a separate input section for the input values. Keep in mind that the formulas in the information section will reference the input cells. You should use absolute and relative cell references, as opposed to constant values.

Test Your Design

After creating the pro forma income statement worksheet, you should test your design. Perform the following steps.

1. Assume sales in 2002 were 2 million, instead of 3.5 million. Now, assume sales in 2002 were 4 million, instead of 3.5 million. What impact, if any, do these changes have? Are there any significant changes in the sales, expenses, or net income?

2. Make the following changes to the percent of sales for the following items. The deli accounts for 7.5 percent of sales; dairy items account for 18.25 percent of sales; canned goods account for 14.38 percent; and frozen food items account for 18.37 percent.

3. Make the following salary changes. Mr. Feronti takes home 12 percent of the gross profit, the sales manager makes $55,000, and the assistant manager makes $42,000. How will these changes impact the grocery mart's net income?

4. Reset your sales percentages and salaries back to their original values and then make the following changes. Assume a discount chain is opening a grocery store in a neighboring town. Mr. Feronti thinks this may cause his sales to decrease. He thinks his growth may decrease in 2003 by 8 percent, 2004 by 3 percent, and 2005 by 1 percent. Would you still recommend renovating the grocery mart? Why or why not?

CASE DELIVERABLES

In order to satisfactorily complete this case, you should build the worksheet as described in the case scenario and then prepare both written and oral presentations. Unless otherwise specified, submit the following deliverables to your professor. Also, unless otherwise specified, perform these steps after you have tested your design.

1. A written report discussing any assumptions you have made about the case and the key elements of the case. Additionally, what features did you add to make the worksheet more functional? User friendly? (Please note that these assumptions cannot violate any of the requirements specified above and must be approved by your professor.)

2. A printout of each worksheet and chart.

3. A printout of the worksheet's formulas.

4. An electronic, working copy of your worksheet that meets the criteria mentioned in the case scenario and specifications sections.

5. Results for each question posed above. (A memo to your instructor discussing these results should also be provided.)

6. As mentioned above, you should prepare an oral presentation. (Your instructor will establish the time allocated to your presentation.) You should use a presentation package and discuss the key features of your worksheet. Also, discuss how the worksheet is beneficial for Mr. Feronti. What additional information should be included in the worksheet to make it more useful?

CASE

4

Terrell & Terrell Property Management, Inc.

Spreadsheet Case   **Difficulty Rating:** ★★

CASE BACKGROUND

Reyna and Rupert Terrell own a small property management business, consisting of two duplexes, three rent houses, and two commercial buildings. As part of their property management business, the Terrells track each unit's income and expenses, as well as the overall income and expenses for their business. Although their existing file management system is adequate, the Terrells want a more flexible property management system that will enable them to monitor and analyze their business's cash flows at varying levels of detail.

The Terrells ask you to prepare a standard cash flow worksheet template that summarizes each rental property's income and expenses, a summary worksheet that summarizes the business's income and expenses from all the rental properties, and several workbooks that will be used to organize the cash flow worksheets. Designing the cash flow worksheets requires you to format cells and worksheets appropriately, use several functions, use 3-D cell references, and work with multiple workbooks.

CASE SCENARIO

Last year Reyna and Rupert Terrell were looking for ways to earn additional retirement income. After locating, purchasing, and renovating several properties in the Crater Lake area, they began renting their properties to the public. The Terrells currently own two duplexes, three rent houses, and two commercial buildings. Although the rental properties generate a modest income for the Terrells, maintaining the properties can be expensive at times, since all units have appliance, property tax, insurance, advertisement, routine maintenance, materials, cable, and labor expenses.

The duplexes, rent houses, and commercial buildings are equipped with major appliances, such as dishwashers, washers, dryers, and refrigerators. When an appliance is no longer repairable, the Terrells replace the appliance and charge the expense to the unit. The Terrells must also pay property tax and insurance for each unit. The property tax is paid once a year, usually in December, and insurance is paid twice a year, generally in July and December. Routine maintenance includes such things as mowing, general landscaping, replacing air filters, cleaning empty rental units, and hauling off trash. When a rental unit requires repairs or routine maintenance, the Terrells record the labor charges, as well as the cost of the materials. Materials include any necessary items used to repair or clean a unit. As an enticement for potential renters, the Terrells pay for basic cable, even for the commercial buildings. When a unit is vacant, the Terrells place an advertisement in the local newspaper and run the advertisement until the unit is rented.

The Terrells use a simple filing system to track each rental unit's income and expenses. Although the filing system provides the Terrells with the necessary income and expense data, analyzing the income and expense data is cumbersome at best. The Terrells realize that using a spreadsheet application will make their property management activities much easier, more efficient, and more accurate. The Terrells ask you to organize their income and expense data into electronic workbooks, so that they can better manage their rental properties.

Design Specifications

The Terrells ask you to create a cash flow worksheet for each rental unit and a summary cash flow worksheet. Since the Terrells want each cash flow worksheet to have a similar look and feel and will use the cash flow worksheet for future properties that they purchase, you decide that a standard cash flow template is necessary. Once you create the standard cash flow template, the Terrells can use the template to enter income and expense data for each rental unit. Figure 1 provides a sketch of a partially completed cash flow worksheet. (Figure 1 shows a cash flow worksheet for six months. Your cash flow worksheet should accommodate 12 months.)

As Figure 1 shows, the cash flow worksheet records the monthly income and expenses for a particular rental unit. Although not shown in Figure 1, the Terrells want to know each month's total expenses, monthly cash flow, overall cash flow, year-to-date total for each expense, and year-to-date total income. The monthly cash flow is the difference between the monthly income and total monthly expenses, and the overall cash flow is a summation of the monthly cash flow up to and including the current month. The year-to-date total for each expense sums the expenses incurred so far that year. The year-to-date total income displays the total income received so far in a given year.

Figure 1: Cash Flow Worksheet

Terrell and Terrell Property Management, Inc. Cash Flow Worksheet (Current Date)						
	1/1/03	2/1/03	3/1/03	4/1/03	5/1/03	6/1/03
Rent						
Expenses						
Labor						
Material						
Advertising						
Cable						
Utilities						
Appliances						
Property						
Insurance						
Routine Maintenance						
Miscellaneous						

The Terrells want the individual cash flow worksheets grouped according to property type. Since they have three main types of rental properties, you create Duplex, House, and Commercial workbooks. After the cash flow worksheets and workbooks are created, you prepare a Summary worksheet and place the Summary worksheet in its own Summary workbook. The Summary worksheet summarizes the income and expense data contained in the other workbooks. The Summary worksheet should show the name of the rental unit, as well as the rental unit's year-to-date income and year-to-date total for each expense category. The Summary worksheet should also show the total expenses and overall cash flow for each property. Since the Summary worksheet must reference data contained in multiple workbooks, you use 3-D cell references in the Summary worksheet to retrieve the necessary data from the other workbooks. (At this point, you may wish to review your system's online help feature to review 3-D cell references.) The Terrells also request that the Summary worksheet resemble the individual cash flow worksheets.

Information Specifications

The Terrells will use the cash flow worksheets to better manage the income and expenses for their rental units. Each individual cash flow worksheet provides information specific to a particular rental unit's monthly income and expenses, year-to-date income and expenses, monthly cash flow, and overall cash flow. In addition to this information, the Terrells request average, minimum, and maximum values for each expense category in the individual cash flow worksheets, as well as the summary worksheet. The Terrells ask you to use data from the Summary worksheet to prepare two charts. The first chart compares the income for each unit, and the second chart compares the overall expenses for each unit. (You may select the chart types.)

In addition to the information requirements specified above, Reyna and Rupert request answers to the following questions. Using the newly designed worksheets, provide Reyna and Rupert with answers to these questions.

1. What was the income from all units last year?

2. On average, how much was spent in each expense category this past year?

3. Based on data contained in the Summary worksheet, where did the Terrells incur the largest expense?

4. What are the total revenues by rental unit category?

5. What are the total expenses by rental unit category?

6. What is the operating income by rental unit category?

7. Should the Terrells raise the rent on any of their properties? Why?

Implementation Concerns

While you are free to work with the design of your worksheets, each worksheet should have a consistent, professional appearance. Also, you should use appropriate formatting for the cells and worksheets. For instance, dollar values should display a dollar sign and be formatted to two decimal places. Since the worksheets have similar categories and contain similar data, you should strive to keep the worksheets' appearances similar.

The Terrells will use the individual cash flow worksheets to maintain the income and expense data for their individual rental property units. The Summary workbook summarizes the data contained in the individual cash flow worksheets. Since the Summary worksheet references external data, you will use 3-D cell references. The syntax for a 3-D cell reference is =[WorkbookName]SheetName!CellAddress. Although you can manually enter a 3-D cell reference into a Summary worksheet cell, it is easier and less error-prone, if you use the point and click method. (For more information about 3-D cell references, use your system's online help feature.)

Test Your Design

After creating the Commercial, Duplex, House, and Summary workbooks, you should test your design. Perform the following steps.

1. Prepare a cash flow worksheet and update the Summary worksheet for the following property.

    The Terrells purchased a duplex and rented one of the duplex units. (The second unit is undergoing renovations.) The duplex unit is located at 1412 Mockingbird and rents for $950.00 a month. November expenses include $2,500.00 in labor, $705.00 in materials, $25.00 in advertising, $84.48 in cable, $98.00 in utilities, $1,050.72 in appliances, and $50.00 in routine maintenance. December expenses include $84.48 in cable, $98.00 in utilities, and $50.00 in routine maintenance. Property taxes and an insurance premium were paid in December. The property taxes are $1,050.00, and the insurance premium is $600.00.

2. The Terrells want a chart comparing the year-to-date income for each rental unit category. (You may choose which chart type to use.)

3. What is the overall cash flow for the rental properties?

CASE DELIVERABLES

In order to satisfactorily complete this case, you should build the workbooks as described in the case scenario and then prepare both written and oral presentations. Unless otherwise specified, submit the following deliverables to your professor. Also, unless otherwise specified, perform these steps after you have tested your design.

1. A written report discussing any assumptions you have made about the case and the key elements of the case. Additionally, what features did you add to make the worksheets and workbooks more functional? User friendly? (Please note that these assumptions cannot violate any of the requirements specified above and must be approved by your professor.)

2. A printout of each worksheet and chart.

3. A printout of each worksheet's formulas.

4. Electronic, working copies of your workbooks that meet the criteria mentioned in the case scenario and specifications sections.

5. Results for each question posed above. (A memo to your instructor discussing these results should also be provided.)

6. As mentioned above, you should prepare an oral presentation. (Your instructor will establish the time allocated to your presentation.) You should use a presentation package and discuss the key features of your worksheets and workbooks. Also, discuss how the worksheets and workbooks are beneficial for Reyna and Rupert. What additional information should be included in the worksheets and workbooks to make them more useful?

CASE 5

Megan Davis Convention Center

Spreadsheet Case　　　**Difficulty Rating:** ★★★

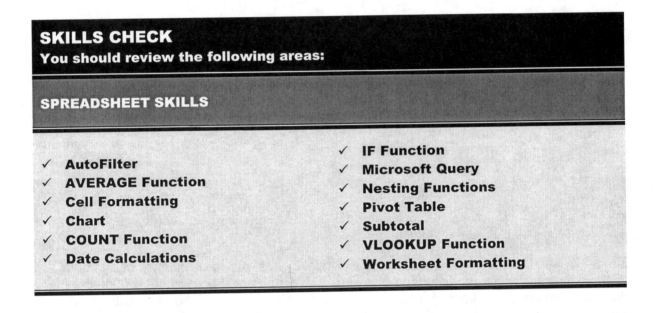

CASE BACKGROUND

The Megan Davis Convention Center, located on the outskirts of a metropolitan area, is a popular attraction for corporate meetings, special events, and educational seminars. The convention center's location, view, facilities, and outstanding reputation attract individuals and corporations from all over the United States. To ensure a reservation, the convention center's clients will often book rooms a year or more in advance.

Mavis Billingsley, the convention center's events coordinator, is responsible for scheduling the meeting rooms and helping the center's clients plan their special events. Ms. Billingsley currently uses the MDCC Reservations database to track the convention center's meeting room reservations. She would like to import the reservation data into a spreadsheet application for analysis. She asks you to import the reservation data into a worksheet, enhance the worksheet by inserting columns, and use the Subtotal, Chart, Pivot Table, and AutoFilter tools to analyze the reservation data.

CASE SCENARIO

As the events coordinator for the Megan Davis Convention Center, Ms. Billingsley is responsible for managing the meeting room reservations. The Megan Davis Convention

Center currently has five standard meeting rooms, a conference center, a boardroom, and an auditorium. A client may book one or all of the rooms. Although the conference center is primarily used for larger meetings, the center can be converted into four smaller meeting rooms, thus providing the convention center with extra meeting rooms. When booking a meeting room, the client may request a particular seating arrangement, such as circular, classroom, lecture, or U-shape. The number of available seats within a given meeting room is dependent upon the seating arrangement. Figure 1 shows the types of seating arrangements and their codes.

Figure 1: Available Seating Arrangements

Megan Davis Convention Center	
Available Seating Arrangements	
Seating Arrangement	**Code**
Circular	CI
Classroom	CL
Lecture	LE
U-Shape	US

Each day, Ms. Billingsley fields calls from potential clients, requesting information about room availability, room capacity, and charges. Convention center clients are quoted either a standard, advanced, or special rate. The standard rate applies to all bookings that are made less than six months in advance. The advanced rate applies to clients who book six months or more in advance, and the special rate is a negotiating tool used to attract large, highly recognizable companies or organizations to the Megan Davis Convention Center. Figure 2 summarizes the meeting room rates.

Figure 2: Meeting Room Rates

Megan Davis Convention Center				
Daily Meeting Room Rates				
Room Code	**Meeting Room**	**Advance Rate**	**Standard Rate**	**Special Rate**
AU	Auditorium	$918.75	$1,225.00	$735.00
BD	Boardroom	$412.50	$550.00	$330.00
CF	Conference Center	$975.00	$1,500.00	$900.00
AL	Alabama	$450.00	$600.00	$390.00
CA	California	$487.50	$650.00	$422.50
CO	Colorado	$468.75	$625.00	$375.00
FL	Florida	$450.00	$600.00	$390.00
GA	Georgia	$431.25	$575.00	$373.75

Design Specifications

The reservation data that Ms. Billingsley needs is currently stored in the Reservation Details table in the MDCC Reservations database. Since Ms. Billingsley will use a spreadsheet application to analyze the reservation data, you import the data into a worksheet for her. As you recall, importing data into a worksheet is easily accomplished by using Microsoft Query. Since Ms. Billingsley will reuse the query to obtain the most current reservation data for analysis, you save the query for future use.

Ms. Billingsley requests that you retrieve all fields from the Reservation Details table. Once you import the reservation data into the worksheet, you realize that the imported reservation data do not include the daily room charge, number of reserved days, or total charges for the clients. Ms. Billingsley explains that these data are not stored in the database, since these values can be looked up or derived from the contents of other database fields. Therefore, it is not necessary for the database to store the daily room charges, number of reserved days, and total charges for each record. Since Ms. Billingsley needs this information for her analysis, you insert the necessary columns into your worksheet.

The Daily Room Charge column specifies the daily meeting room rate that the customer is charged for a particular meeting room. To determine the daily room charge, you must use the room code and assigned rate code to look up how much a client is charged. Determining the value for this column requires using the imported room code and rate code to look up the appropriate rate in a lookup table. Since a lookup table is necessary, you use Figure 2's data to construct your lookup table. You decide that the lookup table may need to be modified in the future, so you decide to place the lookup table in its own worksheet.

The Number of Reserved Days column specifies the number of days that the client reserved the meeting room. Determining the values for this column requires a formula that works with dates. Subtracting the reservation start date from the reservation end date does not give you the correct number of days that the client reserved the room, so you must modify your formula to implement the necessary logic to determine the correct number of reserved days.

The Total Charges column shows the total charges for the meeting room, based on the number of days that the room is reserved by the client. For instance, if a room is rented at $600.00 per day and the client rents the room for 2 days, then the total charges amount is $1,200.00.

Information Specifications

When a client books a meeting room, Ms. Billingsley enters the reservation data into the MDCC Reservations database for processing. Ms. Billingsley knows that the MDCC Reservations database contains important details about her clients' reservations, and she now wants to use a spreadsheet application to analyze the reservation data. Specifically, Ms. Billingsley wants to know how frequently the standard rate is charged, as opposed to the advanced or special rates. She wants a pivot table and chart that compares the count for each rate. (You should select an appropriate chart type.) She wants a count of the seating styles used in each room. She also wants to see the total charges by room.

Ms. Billingsley wants to review the booking habits of the convention center's clients. For instance, she wants to know how far in advance, on average, the center's clients book the meeting rooms. She also wants to know the number of rooms her clients book, as well as the total charges for each client. Additionally, Ms. Billingsley requests that you prepare a chart comparing the revenue by room.

In addition to the information requirements specified above, Ms. Billingsley requests answers to the following questions. Where appropriate, use the Pivot Table, Subtotal, Chart, and AutoFilter tools to provide Ms. Billingsley with answers to her questions.

1. On average, what is the length of time that a client books a room?

2. Using a reservation start date of August 5, 2003, Ms. Billingsley wants to see the total charges for each client.

3. Overall, what is the average daily room charge?

4. Which seating arrangement is most popular?

5. Which reservations were made on February 15, 2003? What are the total charges for the reservations?

6. What are the top five total charges? Which customers are responsible for these total charges?

Implementation Concerns

While you are free to work with the design of your worksheet, it should have a consistent, professional appearance. You should also apply appropriate formatting to the cells and worksheet. For instance, all cells containing dollar values should use a currency format and be formatted to two decimal places. Also, your worksheet should have an appropriate header, as well as appropriate column and row headings.

To prepare your worksheet according to the specifications provided above, you will import external data, insert columns, construct formulas that may include the IF and VLOOKUP functions, work with dates, and use several tools, such as Pivot Table, AutoFilter, Chart, Microsoft Query, and Subtotal.

You can use the Microsoft Query Wizard to import the reservation data. The Microsoft Query Wizard steps you through the process of retrieving external data from the Reservation Details table in the MDCC Reservations database. Keep in mind that the Test Your Design Section requires you to modify the database query and also create a new query to retrieve external data that meet specific criteria. (You may wish to use your system's online help feature to review how to use Microsoft Query and the Microsoft Query Wizard.)

Test Your Design

After creating your worksheet, you should test your design. Perform the following steps.

1. Ms. Billingsley requests that you retrieve **only** the reservation data with a start date of August 12, 2003, from the Reservation Details table. (Hint: This requires modification to your query.)

2. When retrieving data from the Reservation Details table, Ms. Billingsley wants the query to prompt her for a reservation start date. Create a new query that **prompts** Ms. Billingsley for a specific reservation date. Run the query several times and enter different reservation start dates.

CASE DELIVERABLES

In order to satisfactorily complete this case, you should build the worksheets as described in the case scenario and then prepare both written and oral presentations. Unless otherwise specified, submit the following deliverables to your professor. Also, unless otherwise specified, perform these steps after you have tested your design. When preparing the following documentation, use all of the data contained in the Reservation Details table.

1. A written report discussing any assumptions you have made about the case and the key elements of the case. Additionally, what features did you add to make the worksheet(s) more functional? User friendly? (Please note that these assumptions cannot violate any of the requirements specified above and must be approved by your professor.)

2. A printout of each worksheet. (This includes your charts and pivot tables.)

3. A printout of each worksheet's formulas.

4. An electronic, working copy of your workbook that meets the criteria mentioned in the case scenario and specifications sections.

5. Results for each question posed above. (A memo to your instructor discussing these results should also be provided.)

6. As mentioned above, you should prepare an oral presentation. (Your instructor will establish the time allocated to your presentation.) You should use a presentation package and discuss the key features of your workbook. Also, discuss how the workbook is beneficial for Ms. Billingsley. What additional information should be included in the workbook to make it more useful?

CASE BJR Investments, Inc.

6

Spreadsheet Case   **Difficulty Rating:** ★★★

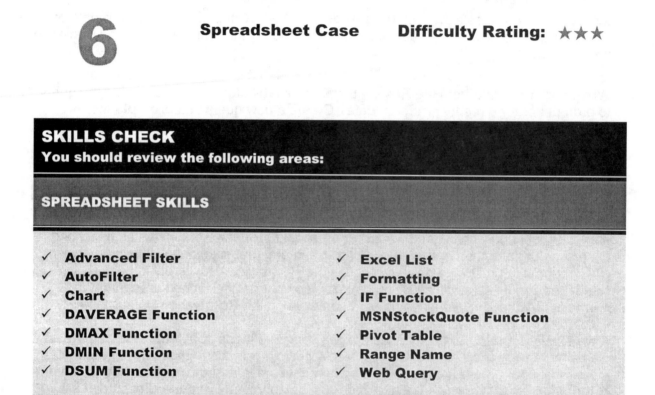

CASE BACKGROUND

BJR Investments, Inc., is a full-service brokerage firm, providing a variety of financial planning services to its current and prospective clients. Bradley J. Reynolds, the owner of BJR Investments, Inc., and his staff provide investment advice in such areas as tax advantage planning, retirement and estate planning, mutual funds, pensions, stocks, and risk management. Mr. Reynolds enjoys helping his clients manage their portfolios, which range in size from $1,000 to well over $3,000,000. His clients appreciate his advice, personal touch, and 15 years of investment experience. However, it is his attention to detail that keeps the business growing.

Mr. Reynolds wants to develop a Portfolio worksheet for each client. He feels that the Portfolio worksheet can provide him with current data about his client's investments, thus helping him keep better track of the client's investments. The Portfolio worksheet organizes the client's stock information into an Excel list and requires the retrieval of up-to-date stock information from the Web. Once current stock information is retrieved, Mr. Reynolds will analyze the information by using the AutoFilter, Advanced Filter, Pivot Table, and PivotChart Report tools.

CASE SCENARIO

Mr. Reynolds asks you to develop a Portfolio worksheet that he will use for each client. The Portfolio worksheet provides Mr. Reynolds with the symbol, company name, industry, and the company's market capitalization, as well as the shares, purchase date, purchase price, commission, total cost, portfolio percentage, current value of the shares, last price, previous close, return, and price-earning (P/E) and earnings-per-share (EPS) ratios for the stock. Since the Portfolio worksheet is organized around the client's investments, Mr. Reynolds can carefully monitor a client's investment activity and provide timely, more accurate advice to the client. Mr. Reynolds thinks his clients will appreciate this special attention to detail.

Once the Portfolio worksheet is developed, Mr. Reynolds will use the Pivot Table, AutoFilter, Advanced Filter, and chart tools to analyze the client's portfolio and provide the best possible advice to the client. Mr. Reynolds will also print a copy of the worksheet, charts, and pivot tables for the client.

Mr. Reynolds is anxious to begin using the worksheet at his firm, and he provides you with a partially completed worksheet for one of his clients. He asks you to complete the Portfolio worksheet for him.

Design Specifications

The partially completed Portfolio worksheet includes symbol, company, industry, number of shares, purchase date, and purchase price columns. The worksheet needs a descriptive title, appropriate column headings, and proper formatting for the cells. You supply a descriptive worksheet title and column headings for the worksheet. Since this worksheet deals with stock information, you decide that the header should show the date, as well as the current time. For cells involving dollar values, you specify a currency format with two decimal places.

For each stock, Mr. Reynolds wants to see the symbol, company name, industry, market capitalization, number of shares, purchase date, purchase price, commission, total cost, portfolio percentage, current value of the shares, last price, previous close, return, P/E ratio, and EPS ratio. Figure 1 provides a sketch of the proposed worksheet (see end of case). As you study the worksheet, you realize that Mr. Reynolds must enter values for the symbol, company, industry, number of shares, purchase date, and purchase price. The values for the remaining columns are retrieved or computed based on the contents of the entered values. The market capitalization, last price, previous close, and EPS values are retrieved from the Web.

The total cost, portfolio percentage, current value, return, commission, and P/E ratio are computed, thus requiring formulas. Figure 2 provides formulas for computing these values. While the total cost, portfolio percentage, current value, and return use simple formulas, you ask Mr. Reynolds to explain how to derive the commission and P/E ratio. Mr. Reynolds explains that he charges either 2 percent of the purchase price or a $25 flat fee, whichever is greater. Based on this explanation, you decide that the commission cells must determine what fee to charge. The determination of what commission to charge requires the use of the IF function. Although the P/E ratio is retrievable from the Web, Mr. Reynolds wants this value computed based on data contained in the worksheet. The P/E ratio computation is easy to make, since a stock's P/E ratio is determined by dividing the stock's last price by the stock's EPS.

Figure 2: Required Portfolio Worksheet Formulas

Portfolio Worksheet Formulas	
Total Cost	(Purchase Price * Number of Shares) + Commission
Portfolio Percentage	$\dfrac{\text{Current Value of the Stock}}{\text{Total Current Value of All Stock}}$
Current Value	Last Price * Number of Shares
Return	$\dfrac{\text{(Current Value of the Stock - Cost of the Stock)}}{\text{Cost of the Stock}}$
P/E Ratio	$\dfrac{\text{Last Price}}{\text{EPS}}$
Commission	Purchase Price + Commission Fee

As you study the requirements for the new worksheet, you realize that the capitalization, last price, previous close, and EPS ratio require current stock market information. Luckily, you recall that the MSNStockQuote function makes retrieval of this information easy. When the MSNStockQuote function is refreshed, it returns the latest available stock information to the cell. You decide to use the MSNStockQuote function to retrieve the capitalization, last price, previous close, and EPS values. Once you obtain the most recent stock market information, you can use formulas to calculate the current value and return. (In addition to the MSNStockQuote function, the MSN MoneyCentral Investor Stock Quotes Web Query retrieves current stock information. Your instructor will specify which feature to use. At this point, you may wish to use your system's online help function to review the MSNStockQuote function and/or the MSN MoneyCentral Investor Stock Quotes Web query.)

Mr. Reynolds requests the averages, minimums, and maximums for the commission, purchase price, current value, return, and P/E ratio columns. Mr. Reynolds wants the minimums and maximums for the portfolio percentages, previous close, and EPS columns. Also, Mr. Reynolds would like to know the total return. Since he will work with this data as a list, he requests that you use database functions, where applicable, to determine the values for these columns.

Information Specifications

Mr. Reynolds will analyze the stock data at varying levels of detail. For instance, he wants to see the return by industry, and he wants a chart comparing the return by industry. Next, he wants to see the return, P/E, and EPS for each stock. He wants this information categorized by industry, and he does not wish to see grand totals. You suggest that he use the PivotTable and PivotChart Report tools for this purpose.

In addition to the information requirements specified above, Mr. Reynolds requests that you perform the following operations. Where appropriate, you should use the Advanced Filter, AutoFilter, and Pivot Table tools.

1. Identify the most expensive stock.

2. Which stock has the highest return? Lowest return?

3. Which stock has the largest P/E ratio? Lowest P/E ratio?

4. Which stock had the highest previous close? Lowest?

5. On which trades did the client pay a $25 flat fee? On which trades did the client pay a 2 percent commission?

6. Which stocks have a purchase price greater than $50 and a negative return?

7. Which stocks have a purchase price less than $50 and a positive return?

8. Identify the purchase price, last price, and previous close for each stock. Mr. Reynolds wants to view this information on a separate "page" for each industry.

Implementation Concerns

While you are free to work with the design of your worksheet, the worksheet should have a consistent, professional appearance. You should also use proper formatting for the cells. For instance, dollar values should display with a dollar sign and be formatted to two decimal places.

To complete the case scenario, your worksheet must retrieve stock information. Although the case scenario suggests using the MSNStockQuote function, you can use the MSN MoneyCentral Investors Stock Quotes Web Query. Since the MSNStockQuote function provides more control over the information that is returned, it is the preferred method. However, the MSNStockQuote function requires the MSN MoneyCentral Stock Quotes add-in. Although this add-in is available at Microsoft's Web site, you may, for a variety of reasons, not have immediate access to the add-in. (Your professor will specify which method to use.) If you elect to use the MoneyCentral Investors Stock Quotes Web Query, you will need to modify your worksheet to accommodate the information that the Web query returns.

The case scenario mentions that the commission fee is based on the purchase price. For each trade, Mr. Reynolds wants to charge either a 2 percent commission or a $25 flat fee, depending on which rate results in a higher commission. Building this logic into the commission cells requires using the IF function. (At this point, you may wish to use your system's online help feature to review the IF function.)

You will need to use the Advanced Filter tool to provide Mr. Reynolds with the information that he needs. The Advanced Filter tool requires a criteria range. As a general rule the criteria range should be placed above or below the Excel list. When filtering data in a list, you should use the DAVERAGE, DMIN, DMAX, and DSUM functions, as opposed to the AVERAGE, MINIMUM, MAXIMUM, and SUM functions. The database functions will accurately reflect the correct average, minimum, maximum, and total values for a filtered list. However, other Excel functions may not. In order for your database functions to work properly, you should create your criteria range before using the database functions.

Test Your Design

After creating the Portfolio worksheet described in the case scenario, you should test your worksheet design. Perform the following operations.

1. Add the following stocks to the Portfolio worksheet. For the purchase date, use today's date. For the purchase price, use the stock's Previous Close value.

New Stocks			
Symbol	Company	Industry	Number of Shares
HDI	Harley-Davidson	Leisure Time	100
HNZ	Heinz	Foods	200
NBR	Nabors Industries	Oil & Gas	50
NCR	NCR Corp.	Computers	200
HSY	Hershey Foods	Foods	100

2. What is the average commission for all stocks? Average P/E ratio for all stocks?

3. For the new stocks that were just purchased, which has the highest return? Lowest? For the new stocks, provide averages for the commission, current value, and P/E ratio. Now, provide the minimums and maximums for the new stocks.

4. Of the large capitalization firms, which has the highest return? P/E ratio? EPS? (Large-capitalization firms have market capitalizations over $5 billion.)

5. Which mid-capitalization firm has the highest current value for its stock? Lowest? (Mid-capitalization firms have market capitalizations between $500 million and $5 billion.)

6. Based on portfolio percentage, identify the top five firms with which the client is invested.

7. Based on the information provided in the Portfolio worksheet, which stock(s) would you recommended eliminating from the portfolio?

CASE DELIVERABLES

In order to satisfactorily complete this case, you should build the worksheet as described in the case scenario and then prepare both written and oral presentations. Unless otherwise specified, submit the following deliverables to your professor. Also, unless otherwise specified, perform these steps after you have tested your design.

1. A written report discussing any assumptions you have made about the case and the key elements of the case. Additionally, what features did you add to make the worksheet(s) more functional? User friendly? (Please note that these assumptions cannot violate any of the requirements specified above and must be approved by your professor.)

2. A printout of each worksheet. (This includes your charts and pivot tables.)

3. A printout of each worksheet's formulas.

4. An electronic, working copy of your workbook that meets the criteria mentioned in the case scenario and specifications sections.

5. Results for each question posed above. (A memo to your instructor discussing these results should also be provided.)

6. As mentioned above, you should prepare an oral presentation. (Your instructor will establish the time allocated to your presentation.) You should use a presentation package and discuss the key features of your workbook. Also, discuss how the workbook is beneficial for Mr. Reynolds. What additional information should be included in the workbook to make it more useful?

Figure 1: Current Investment Worksheet

BJR Investments, Inc.
Portfolio Worksheet
(Current Date and Time)

Symbol	Company	Industry	Capitalization	No. of Shares	Purchase Date	Purchase Price	Commission	Total Cost	Portfolio Percentage	Current Value	Last Price	Previous Close	Return	P/E	EPS

CASE 7

Madison's Department Store

Spreadsheet Case   **Difficulty Rating:** ★★★★

CASE BACKGROUND

Sylvester Tarkio understands the importance of a department store's sales force, especially when it comes to the sales force of a premiere, upscale department store like Madison's. Customers have long enjoyed the expert knowledge, attention to detail, and service that Madison's sales staff provides. Maintaining the quality sales force is a daily job for Mr. Tarkio. He carefully evaluates the performance of his sales staff and makes adjustments when needed. Currently, Mr. Tarkio monitors the performance of his sales staff by reading daily and weekly sales productivity reports. The problem is that these reports are prepared on a word processor. Mr. Tarkio has no efficient way of analyzing the data in detail. As a new intern at Madison's, you have impressed Mr. Tarkio with your work. Mr. Tarkio asks you to prepare a Productivity workbook for him. You will prepare seven daily productivity worksheets and a weekly productivity summary worksheet, analyze the sales data by using the Pivot Table and AutoFilter tools, and generate several charts.

CASE SCENARIO

Madison's Department Store is a prestigious, upscale department store located in one of the metropolitan area malls. The store has specialty departments for women, men, children, cosmetics, cologne, linen, furniture, and housewares. One of the reasons why Madison's has such a fine reputation is because of its highly-trained sales staff. Madison's management believes in rewarding its sales staff for its hard work, so in addition to an hourly wage, sales representatives are paid a commission on sales above an established quota.

Sales representatives are classified as either part-time or full-time. Part-time representatives are then subcategorized as sales assistants or sales partners. Full-time representatives are subcategorized as assistant managers, sales consultants, or sales associates. Part-time representatives work 20 hours a week, while full-time representatives work 40 hours a week. Sales representatives have input into how many hours a day they work; however, they cannot work overtime. Within the company, sales representatives are ranked and paid according to their experience and tenure with the company. Sales representatives are paid a commission on all sales exceeding their established quota. Since members of the sales staff may work a different number of hours on a given day, the sales quota is based on the hours worked. For instance, if a sales representative has an hourly quota of $100 in sales and he works 5 hours, then his daily sales quota is $500. For any sales above the $500 quota, the sales representative receives a commission. Figure 1 summarizes the hourly wages and established quotas.

Figure 1: Hourly Wages and Quotas

Abbreviation	Title	Hourly Wage	Hourly Sales	Commission Rate
AM	Assistant Manager	$20.00	$200.00	.030
PT1	Sales Assistant	$8.50	$100.00	.015
PT2	Sales Partner	$8.75	$125.00	.010
S1	Sales Associate	$10.50	$150.00	.020
S2	Sales Consultant	$12.00	$175.00	.025

At the end of each business day, Mr. Tarkio prepares a Daily Productivity Report. As Figure 2 shows, the Daily Productivity Report summarizes each employee's sales activity for the day. This report specifies the employee's name, rank, assigned department, daily sales, hours, base pay, commission, and gross pay. At the end of each week, Mr. Tarkio uses the Daily Productivity Reports to prepare a Weekly Productivity Report. The Weekly Productivity Report summarizes the Daily Productivity Reports. Mr. Tarkio currently uses a word processor to prepare the reports. However, he realizes that a spreadsheet application is a much better tool for the summarization and analysis work that he needs. Mr. Tarkio asks you to develop a Productivity workbook for him.

Design Specifications

Each day, Mr. Tarkio will enter each salesperson's sales and hours into a Daily Productivity worksheet. He then expects the worksheet to determine each salesperson's base pay, commission, and gross pay. While the gross pay involves adding the base pay to the commission, calculating the base pay and commission requires referencing values in a lookup table. Since you want the lookup table to be easily accessible and updateable, you place the lookup table in its own worksheet.

The base pay and commission are dependent upon the salesperson's rank in the company. For instance, an assistant manager is paid $20 per hour and receives a 3 percent commission. In contrast, a sales associate is paid $10.50 per hour and receives a 2 percent commission. You use the VLOOKUP function to build this logic into the base pay, and you use the IF and VLOOKUP functions to build the logic into the commission cells. The base pay formula uses the salesperson's rank to retrieve the correct hourly wage and then multiplies the hourly wage by the number of hours. The determination of the appropriate commission requires more complicated logic than the base pay. For instance, the commission formula must determine if a commission is to be paid, the applicable commission rate, and the portion of sales on which to base the commission. Since the commission formula involves several lookups and decisions, you realize that nesting the IF and VLOOKUP functions is required. (At this point, you may wish to review your system's online help feature to review the IF and VLOOKUP functions, as well as how to nest functions.)

As previously mentioned, Mr. Tarkio wants the Daily Productivity Reports summarized into a Weekly Productivity Report. The Weekly Productivity Report provides weekly sales, hours, base pay, commission, and gross pay totals for each salesperson. For instance, the sales column will reference and sum the individual sales for Sunday through Saturday.

After showing Mr. Tarkio the workbook prototype, he asks if you can determine the number of times each salesperson made his quota that week. You assure him that the worksheet can be modified to provide this information. On each worksheet, Mr. Tarkio requires grand totals, averages, minimums, and maximums for the sales, base pay, commission, and gross pay columns. Mr. Tarkio wants to see the minimum, maximum, and average for the quotas.

Information Specifications

Mr. Tarkio wants to use the Productivity workbook to analyze the performance of his sales staff. He specifically requests that you show him how to use the Pivot Table and PivotChart Report tools to analyze the sales data. Mr. Tarkio will use these tools to compare the commissions and sales by department, view the commissions by individuals within each department, prepare a pie chart showing the commissions by department, and prepare pie charts for each department, comparing the department's sales representatives' sales.

In addition to the information requirements specified above, Mr. Tarkio wants answers to the following questions. Using the Pivot Table, PivotChart Report, and AutoFilter tools, provide Mr. Tarkio with answers to these questions.

1. Which ten sales representatives received the highest commissions last week?

2. Which sales staff did not make quota this week?

3. For each department, which salesperson had the highest sales?

4. On average, how frequently will the sales staff make their quota?

5. Mr. Tarkio wants to see the commissions and total sales for each sales position by department.

6. Mr. Tarkio wants to see the base pay, commission, and gross pay categorized by sales position.

Implementation Concerns

While you are free to work with the design of your workbook, each worksheet should have a consistent, professional appearance. You should use appropriate formatting for the cells and worksheets.

This case requires you to group worksheets, insert columns into worksheets, consolidate information into a summary worksheet, nest functions, use several functions, reference a lookup table and use the retrieved value in a formula, work with an Excel list, prepare charts, and use several analytical tools to analyze the sales data.

In several instances, you must filter the data contained in the summary worksheet. To provide Mr. Tarkio with correct answers, you should use the DAVERAGE, DMIN, and DMAX functions in the summary worksheet, as opposed to the AVERAGE, MIN, and MAX functions. When data are filtered, the DAVERAGE, DMIN, and DMAX functions adjust their values based on the filtered data. The AVERAGE, MIN, and MAX functions do not.

The determination of each salesperson's commission requires nesting the VLOOKUP function within the IF function. The commission formula must look up the hourly sales quota, determine the daily sales quota, take the difference between the daily sales quota and the daily sales, and then multiply the applicable commission rate by the amount of sales above the quota.

Test Your Design

After creating the Productivity workbook described in the case scenario, you should test your design. Perform the following steps.

1. Mr. Tarkio hired two new sales personnel. Enter their data into the worksheets.

   Leandra Shekel is classified as a PT1 and works in the Men's Clothing Department. She worked 4 hours each day, Sunday through Thursday. Her sales Sunday through Thursday were $1,400.98, $1,500.42, $750.32, $550.08, and $900.78, respectively.

   Darise Ferrer was hired as an S1 and works in the Linen Department. She worked 8-hour shifts, Tuesday through Saturday. Her sales were $2,500.98, $878.23, $1,503.28, $602.98, and $1,304.17, respectively.

2. Which salespersons received more than $1,500 in commissions last week?

3. Based on past performance, what would happen if Mr. Tarkio increased the sales quota for each position by $75 per hour.

4. What would happen if Mr. Tarkio increased each sales position's commission by a quarter of a percent?

CASE DELIVERABLES

In order to satisfactorily complete this case, you should build the workbook as described in the case scenario and then prepare both written and oral presentations. Unless otherwise specified, submit the following deliverables to your professor. Also, unless otherwise specified, perform these steps after you have tested your design.

1. A written report discussing any assumptions you have made about the case and the key elements of the case. Additionally, what features did you add to make the worksheet(s) more functional? User friendly? (Please note that these assumptions cannot violate any of the requirements specified above and must be approved by your professor.)

2. A printout of each worksheet. (This includes your charts and pivot tables.)

3. A printout of each worksheet's formulas.

4. An electronic, working copy of your workbook that meets the criteria mentioned in the case scenario and specifications sections.

5. Results for each question posed above. (A memo to your instructor discussing these results should also be provided.)

6. As mentioned above, you should prepare an oral presentation. (Your instructor will establish the time allocated to your presentation.) You should use a presentation package and discuss the key features of your workbook. Also, discuss how the workbook is beneficial for Mr. Tarkio. What additional information should be included in the workbook to make it more useful?

Figure 2: Daily Productivity Report

Madison's Department Store
Daily Productivity Report
(Current Date)

Employee	Rank	Department	Sales	Hours Worked	Base Pay	Commission	Gross Pay
Allbaugh, Joshua	AM	Cologne	$4,000.00	8.0	$160.00	$72.00	$232.00
Blake, Barney	S2	Cosmetics	$456.76	2.5	$26.50	$3.61	$29.86
Bolyard, Pat	S2	Household	$4,500.00	3.0	$31.50	$103.13	$134.63
.			.	.			
.			.	.			
.			.	.			
Stanton, Catrina	S1	Women's	$25.98	7.0	$84.00	$0.00	$84.00

Baylee Byrd Playsets, Inc.

Spreadsheet Case   **Difficulty Rating:** ★★★★★

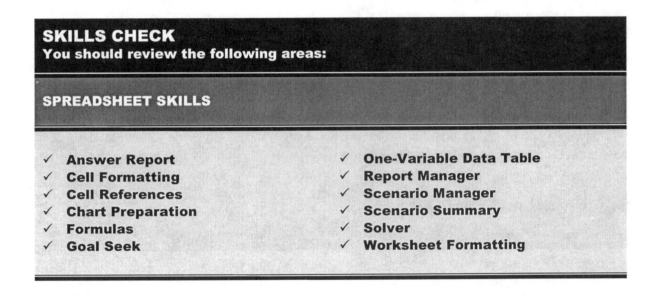

CASE BACKGROUND

A weekend, backyard project that began two years ago has now become a thriving, growing business for Jacob Byrd. Jacob Byrd is the owner and operator of Baylee Byrd Playsets, Inc., a small, part-time business, specializing in the production of quality, custom-built playsets. After friends and neighbors convinced him that he should custom build playsets for their children, Mr. Byrd began his part-time business. Although Mr. Byrd realizes a modest profit from his business, he wants to evaluate the business's operating performance, so that he can determine the best pricing and marketing strategies for his playsets.

Although last year's sales were good, the net income for the business was only $4,183.50. Mr. Byrd feels that his net income should be much higher and has requested your help in evaluating his business's operating performance. To assist Mr. Byrd with the analysis of his business, you will create an income statement, perform breakeven analysis, use several financial ratios, prepare one-variable data tables, use Goal Seek and Solver to perform what-if analysis, prepare a chart, and use the Scenario Manager to prepare different scenarios.

CASE SCENARIO

Two years ago, Jacob Byrd searched for a playset for his four-year-old daughter, Baylee. After spending several months visiting toy and discount stores looking for just the right playset and not finding the perfect one, he decided to custom build a playset for Baylee. The custom-built playset soon became the talk of the town, and Mr. Byrd found himself building playsets for friends and neighbors.

The custom-built playsets are widely recognized throughout the community and in neighboring towns and are an impressive sight. The playsets are made of redwood and equipped with a wave slide, fort, fireman's pole, chin-up bar, safety step ladder, tube slide, bridge, 6' by 6' platform, and two swings.

Last year, Baylee Byrd Playsets, Inc., sold 85 units at $999.99 per unit and generated $84,999.15 in revenue. However, after expenses and taxes were deducted, the business's net income was only $4,183.50. Mr. Byrd would like to improve his net income, and he wonders what he needs to do to achieve this objective. Mr. Byrd needs to evaluate his cash flow to determine areas for improvement and has requested your help.

Design Specifications

After speaking with Mr. Byrd and evaluating his information needs, you decide that an Income Analysis worksheet will help him with his decision-making activities. The Income Analysis worksheet provides Mr. Byrd with several tools for analyzing his business's operating performance. The Income Analysis worksheet enables Mr. Byrd to input the number of units sold, revenue per unit, desired target income, and costs. Once the data are entered, the Income Analysis worksheet provides Mr. Byrd with an income statement, computes financial ratios, performs breakeven analysis, and updates the one-variable data tables.

You determine that the Income Analysis worksheet needs both input and results sections. Figure 1 shows a tentative sketch for the input section. The input section enables Mr. Byrd to input data about the number of units sold, revenue per unit, desired target income, and costs. Table 1 summarizes the company's sales and costs for the previous year.   As you study Table 1's contents, you notice that the costs are separated into two categories: fixed and variable. From a previous business course, you recall that fixed costs remain constant and do not vary with sales volume. Fixed costs for Baylee Byrd Playsets, Inc., include such items as fixed overhead, selling expenses, administrative expenses, and depreciation. In contrast, variable costs change in direct proportion to the sales volume. Variable costs include such items as marketing and sales, labor, variable overhead, variable selling, and variable administrative.

CASE 8: Baylee Byrd Playsets, Inc.

Figure 1: Input Section Sketch

Input Section For Income Analysis Worksheet	
Sales and Cost Summary	
Number of Units Sold	
Revenue Per Unit	
Desired Target Income	
Variable Costs (per unit)	
Marketing and Sales	
Labor	
Variable Overhead	
Variable Selling	
Variable Administrative	
Fixed Costs	
Fixed Overhead	
Selling Expenses	
Administrative Expenses	
Depreciation	

Table 1: Sales and Costs for Previous Year

Income		Fixed Costs	
Units Sold	85	Fixed Overhead	$4,652.11
Price Per Unit	$999.99	Selling Expenses	$2,500.00
Desired Target Income	$30,000.00	Administrative Expenses	$2,399.99
		Depreciation	$7,000.00

Variable Costs (Per Unit)	
Marketing and Sales	$15.24
Labor	$150.00
Variable Overhead	$514.72
Variable Selling	$25.83
Variable Administrative	$23.75

The results section uses the data from the input section to produce an income statement, compute financial ratios, and perform breakeven analysis. The results section will also display your one-variable data tables. (Descriptions for the one-variable data tables are provided in subsequent sections.) Figures 2 provides a sketch for the income statement.

Figure 2: Income Statement

Baylee Byrd Playsets, Inc. Income Statement (Current Date)	
Sales	
Variable Expenses	
Marketing and Sales	
Labor	
Variable Overhead	
Variable Selling	
Variable Administrative	
Total Variable Expenses	
Contribution Margin	
Fixed Expenses	
Fixed Overhead	
Selling Expenses	
Administrative Expenses	
Depreciation	
Total Fixed Expenses	
Operating Income	
Income Taxes	
Net Income	

Information Specifications

The Income Analysis worksheet provides Mr. Byrd with information about his business's income, calculates several financial ratios, performs breakeven analysis, and displays one-variable data tables. Therefore, the Results section of the Income Analysis worksheet will have income statement, ratio, and data table result areas.

As Figure 2 shows, the income statement section of the worksheet summarizes the business's revenues and expenses, allowing Mr. Byrd to examine the company's overall operating performance. As you study the income statement outline, you realize that many of your calculations will reference the data contained in the Input section of the worksheet, requiring Mr. Byrd to input the data only once. Mr. Byrd provides you with the formulas shown in Figure 3.

Mr. Byrd wants to examine the impact that various target income levels have on the breakeven point. For instance, Mr. Byrd knows that a target income of $15,000 requires 117 playsets in order to break even. He would like to see what impact $20,000, $25,000, $30,000, $35,000, and $40,000 target incomes have on the breakeven point. Although he can change the target income cell value for each of the desired target income levels, you recommend that he use a one-variable data table. By creating a one-variable data table, the target income values and their associated breakeven points are arranged in a table, enabling Mr. Byrd to view and compare all the target income values and their associated breakeven points at the same time. (You may wish to use your system's online help feature to review one-variable data tables at this point.)

Figure 3: Required Formulas

Income Analysis Worksheet Formulas	
Breakeven Point	$$\frac{\text{Fixed Costs}}{\text{Revenue Per Unit} - \text{Variable Cost Per Unit}}$$
Breakeven Point With Target Income	$$\frac{\text{Fixed Costs} + \text{Target Income}}{\text{Revenue Per Unit} - \text{Variable Cost Per Unit}}$$
Contribution Margin	Sales – Total Variable Expenses
Contribution Margin Ratio	$$\frac{\text{Sales} - \text{Variable Cost}}{\text{Sales}}$$
Income Taxes (Assume a 35 percent tax rate)	Operating Income * Income Tax Rate
Net Income	Operating Income – Income Taxes
Net Margin	$$\frac{\text{Net Income}}{\text{Net Sales}}$$
Operating Income	Contribution Margin – Total Fixed Expenses
Operating Margin	$$\frac{\text{Operating Income}}{\text{Net Sales}}$$
Variable Cost Per Unit	$$\frac{\text{Total Variable Costs}}{\text{Number of Units Sold}}$$

Mr. Byrd wants to see how different scenarios impact the business's net income. In addition to the current scenario, Mr. Byrd wants to evaluate two other possible scenarios. In the first scenario, he wants to increase the number of units sold to 150, decrease revenue per unit to $950, and decrease variable costs per unit by $10. (You can choose which variable cost to reduce.) In the second scenario, he wants to increase the number of units sold to 100, increase revenue to $1,050 per unit, and increase labor by $50. Using Scenario Manager, you prepare the three scenarios. The first scenario uses the original values, and the remaining two scenarios use the data that Mr. Byrd has just given you. After you create the three scenarios, you generate a scenario summary report based on the three scenarios.

Mr. Byrd needs answers to the following questions. Using your newly designed Income Analysis worksheet, provide Mr. Byrd with answers to his questions.

1. Mr. Byrd wants a net margin ratio of 15 percent. Using Solver, adjust the values for the revenue and number of units sold. Revenue per unit cannot exceed $1,100, the number of units sold cannot exceed 250, and total variable expenses cannot exceed $110,000. In order to have a net margin of 15 percent, how many playsets will Mr. Byrd need to sell? What price should he charge? Generate an answer report. (As a starting point for this answer, reset your worksheet's values back to the original values in Table 1, and then make the changes requested in this question.)

2. Assume that fixed overhead costs are $7,500, variable overhead is $375, labor is $200, and depreciation is $8,500. If Mr. Byrd wants a net income of $30,000, what price should Mr. Byrd charge for his playsets? How many playsets should Mr. Byrd sell? (As a starting point for this answer, reset your worksheet's values back to the original values in Table 1, and then make the changes requested in this question.)

3. Mr. Byrd wants a net income of $55,000. How many playsets should Mr. Byrd sell? What price should he charge? (As a starting point for this answer, reset your worksheet's values back to the original values in Table 1, and then make the changes requested in this question.)

4. Mr. Byrd needs a 3-D pie chart that compares the business's fixed costs.

Implementation Concerns

For this case, you will design a worksheet to facilitate Mr. Byrd's analysis of his business. When designing the worksheet, you will apply basic cell and worksheet formatting principles, create formulas, perform what-if analysis by using Goal Seek and Solver, create several scenarios, generate a chart, and create two one-variable data tables. Based on your what-if analysis, you will prepare several reports, including an answer report and a scenario summary report.

While you are free to work with the design of your worksheet, the worksheet should have a consistent, professional appearance. You should use proper formatting for the cells. For instance, dollar values should display with a dollar sign and be formatted to two decimal places.

In several locations, the case references target income. Keep in mind that the target income does not reflect income taxes. Therefore, as it is used in this case, the target income is a better reflection of operating income, as opposed to net income.

Test Your Design

1. Assume that fixed overhead is $5,000, selling expenses are $4,500, administrative expenses are $3,000, and labor costs are $250. What is Mr. Byrd's net income? (As a starting point for this answer, reset your worksheet's values back to the original values in Table 1, and then make the changes requested in this question.)

2. In order to have a net income of $20,000, how many playsets must Mr. Byrd sell? What price should he charge for the playsets? (As a starting point for this answer, reset your worksheet's values back to the original values in Table 1, and then make the changes requested in this question.)

3. Mr. Byrd wants to identify the breakeven point and breakeven point with target income for varying pricing levels. Prepare a one-variable data table that shows this information. The pricing levels range from $800 to $1,200, in $10 increments. If Mr. Byrd does not want to sell more than 120 playsets and wants to have a $30,000 net income, how many units must he sell? (As a starting point for this answer, reset your worksheet's values back to the original values in Table 1, and then make the changes requested in this question.)

CASE DELIVERABLES

In order to satisfactorily complete this case, you should build the worksheet as described in the case scenario and then prepare both written and oral presentations. Unless otherwise specified, submit the following deliverables to your professor. Also, unless otherwise specified, perform these steps after you have tested your design.

1. A written report discussing any assumptions you have made about the case and the key elements of the case. Additionally, what features did you add to make the worksheet more functional? User friendly? (Please note that these assumptions cannot violate any of the requirements specified above and must be approved by your professor.)

2. A printout of each worksheet and report.

3. An electronic, working copy of your worksheet that meets the criteria mentioned in the case scenario and specifications sections.

4. Results for each question posed above. (A memo to your instructor discussing these results should also be provided.)

5. As mentioned above, you should prepare an oral presentation. (Your instructor will establish the time allocated to your presentation.) You should use a presentation package and discuss the key features of your worksheet. Also, discuss how the worksheet is beneficial for Mr. Byrd. What additional information should be included in the worksheet to make it more useful?

CASE 9

Edmund Grant Pharmaceutical Company

Spreadsheet Case **Difficulty Rating:** ★★★★★

SKILLS CHECK
You should review the following areas:

SPREADSHEET SKILLS

- ✓ Access Form
- ✓ Advanced Filter
- ✓ AutoFilter
- ✓ Button
- ✓ Cell Formatting
- ✓ Conditional Formatting
- ✓ Formulas
- ✓ DAVERAGE Function
- ✓ DMAX Function
- ✓ DMIN Function

- ✓ DSUM Function
- ✓ IF Function
- ✓ Excel List
- ✓ Macro
- ✓ Nesting Functions
- ✓ PivotChart Report
- ✓ Pivot Table
- ✓ Template
- ✓ VLOOKUP Function
- ✓ Worksheet Formatting

CASE BACKGROUND

Keiko Lapeer is a district sales manager for the Edmund Grant Pharmaceutical Company. Ms. Lapeer has many responsibilities, including traveling, visiting with current and potential customers, supervising a growing sales staff, preparing numerous reports, and tracking her sales region's expenses. Each week, members of Ms. Lapeer's sales staff submit weekly expense claim forms. Currently, she scans through the expense forms, checks for anything out of the ordinary, and then authorizes reimbursement checks. Ms. Lapeer needs to become more organized about tracking her sales staff's expenses, and asks you to design an Expense worksheet for her. Specifically, she requests you to organize the expense data into an Excel list. To design the worksheet according to Ms. Lapeer's specifications, you are required to use database functions, use other Excel functions and nest functions. You will then use the AutoFilter, Advanced Filter, Pivot Table, and charting tools to analyze the data.

CASE SCENARIO

The Edmund Grant Pharmaceutical Company (EGPC) is a multinational company, well-known in the United States for its anti-infective, wound care, and pain management products. The Edmund Grant Pharmaceutical Company's sales force is responsible for promoting EGPC products to doctors, pharmacists, and opticians around the globe. Keiko Lapeer is one of EGPC's many district sales managers and is responsible for supervising four sales areas.

As a district sales manager, Ms. Lapeer stays very busy. She often travels, attends several meetings a month, visits with customers, supervises a 23 member sales force, and performs managerial duties. As a manager, Ms. Lapeer's paperwork is often overwhelming, and she is looking for avenues of improvement. One area for improvement is the expense tracking of her sales force. She can easily spend an entire day just processing budget and expense reports. By using a spreadsheet application to analyze her sales force's expenses, she feels that she will save time and make better decisions.

Sales representatives are reimbursed for business meals and calls, gas, hotel, airfare, and other miscellaneous expenses. Each week, sales representatives complete expense claim forms and submit these forms to Ms. Lapeer. Figure 1 provides an example of the expense claim form. Ms. Lapeer summarizes the expense data contained on these forms and prepares several weekly reports. Report preparation is a tedious, time-consuming task, often requiring her to wade through the expense claim forms numerous times.

Figure 1: Expense Claim Form

Edmund Grant Pharmaceutical Company

Expense Claim Form

Employee Name:_____   For Week Ending: _____
Division Number: _____

Expense

Meals:_____
Phone: _____
Gas: _____
Hotel: _____
Airfare: _____
Miscellaneous: _____
_____
_____
_____
Total Expenses Claimed: _____

Mileage

Beginning Mileage: _____
Ending Mileage: _____

Comments: _____
_____
_____
_____
_____

Notice: All expense claims must be accompanied by receipts.

When a sales representative is hired, he is issued a company car. The sales representative may use his car for both business and personal travel, and he is given a weekly mileage limit. Each week, the sales representative reports the number of miles that he drove his car that week. For any miles over the mileage limit, the employee is charged an overage fee. The allowable mileage and charge rate vary by sales position within the company. Table 1 summarizes the allowable mileage and charge rates. Ms. Lapeer wants the new Expense worksheet to determine the mileage overage amount and applicable charges for each sales representative.

Table 1: Allowable Mileage and Rates

Edmund Grant Pharmaceutical Company Allowable Mileage and Rates		
Position	Allowable Miles	Rate
MN	700	0.20
SU	600	0.22
S2	550	0.25
S1	500	0.32

When a car has 60,000 miles, the sales representative can request a new car. Ms. Lapeer wonders if there is some way that she can quickly determine when a car is reaching its end-of-service date. You recommend using conditional formatting to highlight ending mileage readings that are greater than 55,000 miles. If a sales representative has a car that is approaching its end-of-service date, Ms. Lapeer can remind the sales representative that it is time to request a new car.

Ms. Lapeer has used a spreadsheet application before and would like to organize the weekly expense data into a worksheet. She asks you to create an Expense worksheet for her. She specifically requests that you prepare an Excel list, establish a criteria range to support Advanced Filtering, include several database functions, insert four new columns, prepare pivot tables, and prepare several charts. Ms. Lapeer also requests that the new worksheet be saved as a template, so she can reuse it each week.

Design Specifications

As you examine the Expense worksheet, you realize that the worksheet columns need formatting. After formatting the columns, you decide that a mileage lookup table and four additional columns are necessary. Before inserting the four columns, you build the mileage lookup table. Since you want to keep the mileage lookup table separate from the expense data, you place the table in its own worksheet. After creating the mileage lookup table, you insert the actual mileage, overage, overage charge, and total expense columns into the Expense worksheet. The actual mileage column calculates the actual miles that each employee drove during the week. Actual mileage is the difference between the week's ending mileage and the week's beginning mileage. You want the overage column to reference the mileage lookup table and then determine how many miles over the limit, if any, the employee has driven. (Performing this operation requires nesting IF and VLOOKUP functions. At this point, you may wish to use your system's online help feature to review how to nest functions.) The overage charge column uses the VLOOKUP function as well. This column multiplies the overage by the rate specified in the mileage table. The total expenses column is a summation of the expenses for that week.

Ms. Lapeer will use the Advanced Filter capability. Using the Advanced Filter requires the inclusion of a criteria range. For Ms. Lapeer's purposes, you decide the best place for the criteria range is above the data list. (At this point, you may wish to use your system's online help feature to review the Advanced Filter topic.) As Ms. Lapeer uses the criteria range, she needs to clear the range of the current conditions and enter new conditions in the criteria range. You decide to create a macro that will clear the criteria range and position the pointer in the upper left-hand cell of the criteria range. Once you have created the macro, you then assign it to a button named "Clear Criteria."

As you study the contents of the Expense worksheet, you realize that the contents are in a format suitable for creating an Excel list. You recall from one of your business courses that an Excel list is a collection of data, similar in concept to a database table. The data in this Excel list can be filtered, sorted, and manipulated in a variety of ways, thus facilitating Ms. Lapeer's decision-making activities. In fact, several database functions are available for usage with an Excel list, and you decide to use these functions in the Expense worksheet. Ms. Lapeer wants average, minimum, maximum, and total values for the meal, actual mileage, phone, gas, hotel, miscellaneous, airfare, overage, overage charge, and total expense columns in the list. Since Ms. Lapeer will manipulate the data in the list, you use the DAVERAGE, DMIN, DMAX, and DSUM functions. (At this point, you may wish to use your system's online help feature to review list creation and usage.)

Since the expense list has many columns, you want to facilitate the data entry process by using a form. As you recall, you can create a form using either Microsoft Excel or Microsoft Access. The Microsoft Excel data entry form has a simplistic appearance and is not very appealing to the eye. In contrast, Microsoft Access provides more control over the form's design, so you decide to use Microsoft Access to create the data entry form. (Your professor will indicate which type of form to use.)

After you design the worksheet, Ms. Lapeer wants a template created. Then each week, she can use the template to create a worksheet for that week.

Information Specifications

Ms. Lapeer asks if it is possible to view the expense data at varying levels of detail and from different perspectives. She specifically requests a summary of all expenses categorized by division, the total expenses displayed by sales position and the total expenses for the meals, phone and gas expense categories by division and position. Since the pivot table tool can quickly change the way data display and the level of summarization, you recommend that Ms. Lapeer use a pivot table.

As mentioned previously, Ms. Lapeer wants to know when a salesperson's car is approaching 60,000 miles. For any vehicle that has more than 55,000 miles, the spreadsheet application should highlight the ending mileage for that vehicle.

In addition to the information requirements specified above, Ms. Lapeer requests that you perform the following operations.

1. Identify which managers claimed airfare expenses totaling more than $700 and which supervisors claimed airfare expenses totaling more than $500.

2. Which sales representative(s) did not submit an expense claim form?

3. Ms. Lapeer wants to know the hotel and airfare expenses by position.

4. Which managers traveled via airplane during the week?

5. She wants a count of the sales positions by division.

6. Ms. Lapeer wants to know which division had the lowest expenses for the week.

7. Which S1 sales representative(s) submitted hotel and airfare expenses this past week?

8. She wants to know which individuals went over their mileage limits.

Implementation Concerns

While you are free to work with the design of your worksheet, it should have a consistent, professional appearance. You should also use proper formatting for the cells. For instance, dollar values should display with a dollar sign and be formatted to two decimal places.

This case scenario requires you to use an Excel list. Extracting the data requires you to prepare charts; use the DAVERAGE, DSUM, DMIN, DMAX, IF, and VLOOKUP functions; nest functions; establish a criteria range; prepare pivot tables and charts; and use AutoFilter and Advanced Filter. (You may wish to use your system's online help feature to review each of these areas.)

The Design section requires you to prepare a form, either a data entry form or an Access form. (Your professor will provide instructions on which type of form to use.) The Access form requires an add-in, so you may not have this feature readily available. However, using the Access form is well worth the effort, since it provides you with the capability of actually designing a data entry form for Ms. Lapeer.

The determination of the overage amount for each salesperson requires the spreadsheet application to look up the mileage allowance, determine if the mileage is greater than the allowance, and then compute the actual overage amount, if any. Performance of this task requires nesting the VLOOKUP function inside the IF function. (At this point, you may wish to use your system's online help feature to review nesting functions.) Keep in mind that Ms. Lapeer wants the mileage overage amount to display in one column.

You should carefully consider the placement of the criteria range and the mileage table. It is generally recommended that the criteria range be placed above or below the data list. Placement of the criteria range in either of these locations facilitates the viewing of the criteria and the filter results. Although your mileage lookup table may be placed in the Expense worksheet, consider placing the lookup table in its own worksheet. Using a separate worksheet for the mileage lookup table facilitates table maintenance and accessibility.

Test Your Design

After creating the Expense worksheet described in the case scenario, you should test your worksheet design. Perform the following operations.

1. Add the following two new employees to your data list.

Employee 1	Employee 2
Last Name: Ruokangas **First Name:** Leota	**Last Name:** Saghafi **First Name:** Abduellah
Division: 1 **Position:** MN	**Division:** 3 **Position:** S1
Meals: $376.89 **Phone:**$79.86 **Hotel:** $478.78 **Miscellaneous:** $2,987.42 **Airfare:** $894.87	**Meals:** $102.78 **Phone:** $10.07 **Hotel:** $0.00 **Miscellaneous:**$0.00 **Airfare:** $0.00
Beginning Mileage: 101 **Ending Mileage:** 372	**Beginning Mileage:** 904 **Ending Mileage:** 1,150

2. Make the following changes to your mileage table.

Allowable Mileage Table		
Position	Allowable Miles	Rate
MN	700	0.25
SU	600	0.28
S2	550	0.30
S1	500	0.32

3. Within each division, Ms. Lapeer wants to examine the expenses incurred by each employee. She would like to view the divisions one "page" at a time.

4. Prepare a column chart that compares the gas, hotel, airfare, and meal expenses for each division.

5. For each division, Ms. Lapeer wants to see the person's last name and the number of miles he drove last week. She would like to see a grand total for each division. Prepare a pivot table and also prepare a chart for Division 1. (Choose an appropriate chart.)

CASE DELIVERABLES

In order to satisfactorily complete this case, you should build the workbook as described in the case scenario and then prepare both written and oral presentations. Unless otherwise specified, submit the following deliverables to your professor. Also, unless otherwise specified, perform these steps after you have tested your design.

1. A written report discussing any assumptions you have made about the case and the key elements of the case. Additionally, what features did you add to make the worksheets more functional? User friendly? (Please note that these assumptions cannot violate any of the requirements specified above and must be approved by your professor.)

2. A printout of each worksheet. (This includes your charts and pivot tables.)

3. A printout of each worksheet's formulas.

4. An electronic, working copy of your workbook that meets the criteria mentioned in the case scenario and specifications sections.

5. Results for each question posed above. (A memo to your instructor discussing these results should also be provided.)

6. As mentioned above, you should prepare an oral presentation. (Your instructor will establish the time allocated to your presentation.) You should use a presentation package and discuss the key features of your workbook. Also, discuss how the workbook is beneficial for Ms. Lapeer. What additional information should be included in the workbook to make it more useful?

CASE
10

KoKo's Canine Pet Club

Database Case   **Difficulty Rating:** ★

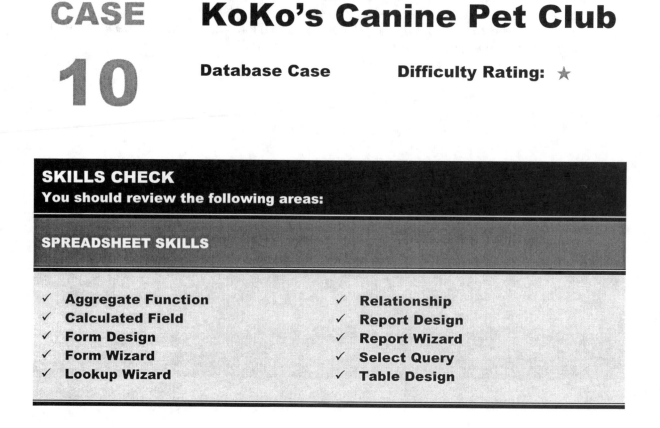

SKILLS CHECK

You should review the following areas:

SPREADSHEET SKILLS

- ✓ Aggregate Function
- ✓ Calculated Field
- ✓ Form Design
- ✓ Form Wizard
- ✓ Lookup Wizard

- ✓ Relationship
- ✓ Report Design
- ✓ Report Wizard
- ✓ Select Query
- ✓ Table Design

CASE BACKGROUND

Six months ago, Caedee Hannah found herself facing a dilemma. As a result of a chronic illness, KoKo, her beloved schnauzer required medication, a special diet, and daily exercise. While the medication and special diet were easy to accommodate into a busy life style, ensuring that KoKo received daily exercise was another matter. Although KoKo's daily exercise usually took the form of a walk around the neighborhood, Caedee, as a busy executive, had trouble scheduling KoKo's daily walks. Caedee's friend, Ian, would walk KoKo on the days when Caedee was extremely busy. Caedee's friends and neighbors liked the pet walking idea so much that they approached Caedee and Ian about walking their dogs as well. What began as a neighborhood walking service, has now become a fledgling, yet growing, metropolitan area business. Ms. Hannah has hired you to build a simple, yet effective, database for her business. She needs you to build Client and Pet forms, Client and Pet tables, Walker Schedule and Client List reports, and several queries.

CASE SCENARIO

KoKo's Canine Pet Club is a dog-walking service, catering to caring, yet busy, pet owners. The service proves very popular with pet lovers who recognize the value of providing their pets with daily exercise. Although the service was only started six months ago, it currently provides pet walking services for 50 pets and is registering, on average, 5 pets per week. Paperwork is increasing, and Caedee Hannah, the service's owner, needs a better record keeping system.

During a meeting with Ms. Hannah, she explains to you that a new client must register with the service. During the registration process, the new client provides basic information about his pet(s), chooses a preferred walk time for his pet(s) and specifies a walker preference. During this time, a dog-walking fee is determined and recorded on the pet registration form. The dog-walking fee varies by pet and is based on the pet's size, temperament, and the number of pets the owner has. The pet owner can request that his pet be walked in the early morning, late morning, early afternoon, late afternoon, or early evening hours. Available walk times are currently kept on a clipboard by the phone. However, Caedee wants the available walk times, as well as walker, client, and pet information, kept in the database that you are building.

Caedee's record keeping needs are simple. She requires a database that tracks her clients, their pets, available walk times, and the pet walkers. Caedee gives you a partially completed database and requests that you build and populate Client and Pet tables, create several relationships, design Client and Pet forms, design Walker Schedule and Client List reports, and construct several queries.

Storage Specifications

After reviewing the partially completed KoKo's Canine Pet Club database, you notice that the database currently contains Walker and Walk tables. The Walker table stores basic information about each walker, and the WalkerNo field serves as the table's primary key. The Walk table stores a set of walk time codes. When a client registers a pet, a walk time code is assigned to each pet. This walk time code indicates the pet owner's preference for the time of day when the pet should be walked.

KoKo's Canine Pet Club database requires both Client and Pet tables. You decide the Client table should store contact information for each client and that the client identification number should serve as the primary key. Table 1 shows the structure for the Client table. (Your instructor will provide you with the data to populate the Client table.)

The Pet table stores information about each pet, including the pet number, pet name, client identification number, walker identification number, quoted price, preferred walk time, enrollment date, and any relevant comments. Table 2 shows the structure for the Pet table. (Your instructor will provide you with the data to populate the Pet table.) As you study this structure, you notice that the WalkerNo and WalkTimeCode fields are part of the Pet table structure. Since the WalkerNo and WalkTimeCode fields already exist in other tables, you use the Lookup Wizard to create these fields in the Pet table. By using the Lookup Wizard, you can facilitate data entry and ensure accuracy for both fields. (The Lookup Wizard is invoked when you select the Lookup Wizard as the data type for the field.)

Table 1: Client Table Structure

Field Name	Data Type	Field Description	Field Size	Comments
ClientNo	AutoNumber	Is a unique, identifying number assigned to each client. Serves as primary key.	Long Integer	Is required.
CLastName	Text	Is the customer's last name.	50	Is required.
CFirstName	Text	Is the customer's first name.	25	Is required.
CAddress	Text	Is the customer's street address.	25	Is required.
CCity	Text	Is the customer's city.	25	Is required.
CState	Text	Is the customer's state abbreviation. The default is OK.	2	Is required.
CZip	Text	Is the customer's zip code. Use an input mask.	10	Is required.
CPhone	Text	Is the customer's home phone number. Use for nonemergency contact. Use an input mask.	8	Is required.
EPhone	Text	Is the customer's emergency phone number. Use for emergency contact. Use an input mask.	8	Is required.

Table 2: Pet Table Structure

Field Name	Data Type	Field Description	Field Size	Comments
PetNo	Text	Is a unique identification number assigned to each pet. Serves as primary key.	10	Is required.
PetName	Text	Stores the pet's name.	25	Is required.
ClientNo	Text	Is the client identification number. Must match a client number from the Client table. Use the Lookup Wizard.	4	Is required.

Field Name	Data Type	Field Description	Field Size	Comments
WalkerNo	Text	Is the walker identification number. Must match a walker identification number from the Walker table. Use the Lookup Wizard.	4	Is required.
QuotedPrice	Currency	Stores the daily walk fee. Caedee determines the actual price per pet.	8	Is required.
WalkTimeCode	Text	Is the code designating the preferred time for walking the pet. Use the Lookup Wizard.	2	Is required.
EnrollmentDate	Date/Time	Indicates when the client enrolled the pet. Use the short date format.	8	Is required.
Comments	Memo	Contains any additional information that is necessary.		

After studying your notes, you decide three relationships are necessary. First, a relationship between the Pet and Client tables is needed. Since each table contains a ClientNo field, you use the ClientNo field to create the relationship. Second, a relationship between the Walker and Pet tables is necessary. The Walker and Pet tables have a WalkerNo field, and you use this field to create a relationship between the Walker and Pet tables. Third, both the Walk and Pet tables have a WalkTimeCode field. You use the WalkTimeCode field to create the relationship between the Walk and Pet tables. You decide each relationship should enforce referential integrity. (Note: The Lookup Wizard will create relationships for you. However, you need to edit these relationships to enforce referential integrity.)

Input Specifications

Figure 1 provides a tentative sketch for the Client form that Caedee wants to use. When a new client enrolls his pet with the walking service, Caedee uses this form to capture contact information about the client, such as his name, address, and phone number. As the tentative sketch shows, the form header includes the service's name, the form's name, and graphics. After studying the tentative sketch, you use the Form Wizard to build an initial Pet form. Once the form is built, you edit the form in Design view.

Figure 1: Client Form

KoKo's Canine Pet Club

Client

Client No:	Street Address:
Client Last Name:	City:
Client First Name:	State: Zip:
Client Phone:	
Emergency Phone:	

After a client registers, Caedee enrolls his pet(s). The pet enrollment process is simple and captures basic information about the pet, such as the pet's name, walk time, and walker preference. You use the Form Wizard to build the initial Pet form. Once the initial form is built, you edit the form in Design View.

Figure 2: Pet Form

KoKo's Canine Pet Club

Pet

Client No: Walker No:

Pet No: Walk Time Code:

Pet Name:

Enrollment Date: Quoted Price:

Comments:

Information Specifications

Caedee requests Walker Schedule and Client List reports. The Walker Schedule report is generated on a weekly basis and tells Caedee when her walkers are scheduled to walk the pets. Since the Walker Schedule report uses data from four tables, you build a select query, and then base the report on the select query. As the tentative sketch in Figure 3 shows, the Walker Schedule report header contains the service's name, a report title, the current date, and graphics. The information in the report body lists the walkers in ascending order based on the walker's last name. A secondary sort is performed on the walk time code, and within the walk time code category, the information is sorted based on the client's last name. Caedee also mentions that she wants the Walker Schedule report to utilize a landscape orientation.

Figure 4 shows a tentative sketch for the Client List report. The Client List report provides a listing of the service's current clients. You use the Report Wizard to speed initial report development, and then edit this report in Design view. The Client List report's header contains the service's name, report name, current date, and graphics. To maintain a consistent appearance with the Walker Schedule report, you use a report style similar to the Walker Schedule report.

Figure 3: Walker Schedule

KoKo's Canine Pet Club

Walker Schedule

(Current Date)

Last Name	Code	Client	Pet Name	Address	City	Phone	E-Phone
Jordan	3	Monac	Bear	303 Northridge	Edmond	899-2395	909-8679
	3	Stone	Bruno	1408 Peter Pan Drive	Yukon	899-8182	606-3402
				.			
				.			
				.			
Morgan	1	Ruaz	Molly	1701 Memorial Road	Oklahoma City	905-8440	606-4102
				.			
				.			
				.			

Figure 4: Client List Report

KoKo's Canine Pet Club

Client List

(Current Date)

Client Name	Address	City	Phone
Blake, Barney	101 Sunnyville Lane	Edmond	606-8975
		.	
		.	
		.	
Stone, David	1408 Peter Pan Drive	Yukon	899-8182
		.	
		. .	
		.	

Ms. Hannah needs answers to the following questions. Build queries to help Ms. Hannah answer these questions. If you choose, you may generate reports based on these queries.

1. How many pets does each pet walker currently walk? Show the walker's first and last name and the pet count for each pet walker. Sort the information in ascending order based on the pet walker's last name.

2. Which clients are located in Edmond? Provide their last and first names.

3. Which clients have three or more pets? Show each client's first and last name and the number of pets he currently has.

4. What are the total pet walking fees charged to each client? Show the client's first and last name and the total fees charged to him.

5. Which pets does Bob walk in the early morning? For each pet, show the pet's name, his owner's last name, and his owner's phone number.

Implementation Concerns

While you are free to work with the design of the forms and reports, each form and report should have a consistent, professional appearance. Consider using the wizards to prepare the initial forms and reports. Once you have prepared the initial forms and reports, you can edit them in Design view.

A lookup field enables the end user to select a value from a list, thus facilitating data entry and promoting data accuracy. You should define the ClientNo, WalkerNo, and WalkTimeCode fields in the Pet table as lookup fields. When defining the data type for each field, select the Lookup Wizard in the Data Type column and follow the directions in the Lookup Wizard dialogue boxes.

Test Your Design

After creating the forms, tables, relationships, queries, and reports, you should test your database design. Perform the following steps.

1. In addition to the pet walker's base pay, Ms. Hannah wants to give each pet walker a 10 percent commission for each pet that he walks. The commission is based on the fee charged to walk the pet. What is the total commission for each pet walker? Provide the walker's first and last name and his total commission.

2. Ms. Hannah wants to know the number of clients she has in each town. Provide the name of the town and the number of clients for each town.

3. Ms. Hannah is considering raising her fees. She would like to raise the fee for the most popular time. Which walk time is most popular? Provide the walk time description and a count of the number of pets walked at that time.

4. On average, how much does Ms. Hannah charge her clients for walking their pets? Show only the average.

5. Two new clients have enrolled with the pet walking service. Enter their information, along with the information about their pets, into the database. For each client, assign the next available client identification number. For each pet, assign the next available pet identification number. For each pet, add any comments that you feel are necessary.

   Fancy Tibbs lives at 48473 Roosevelt Drive in Luther, Oklahoma. The zip code is 73002; her phone number is 943-8789, and her emergency number is 910-5746. Mickey, Precious, Prancer, and Spot are her four pets. Mickey is a Yorkshire terrier, Precious is a poodle, Prancer is a Daschund, and Spot is a Dalmatian. The three small dogs cost $6.50 to walk, and the larger dog costs $8.50 to walk. Ms. Tibbs wants Bob Legier to walk each dog in the early morning. The enrollment date is 10/28/2003.

   Thunder Dumont lives at 84739 Park Lane in Guthrie, OK. The zip code is 73250; his phone number is 748-0098, and his emergency number is 748-9876. Mr. Dumont has two pets. Lightning is a poodle and costs $4.50 to walk. Sunshine is a Great Dane and costs $8.50 to walk. Mr. Dumont requests that Kelly Lamont walk his dogs in the late afternoon. The enrollment date is 11/1/2003.

CASE DELIVERABLES

In order to satisfactorily complete this case, you should build the database and then prepare both written and oral presentations. Unless otherwise specified, submit the following deliverables to your professor. Also, unless otherwise specified, perform these steps after you have tested your design.

1. A written report discussing any assumptions you have made about the case and the key elements of the case. Additionally, what features did you add to make the database more functional? User friendly? (Please note that these assumptions cannot violate any of the requirements specified above and must be approved by your professor.)

2. A printout of each form.

3. A printout of each report.

4. An electronic, working copy of your database that meets the criteria mentioned in the case scenario and specifications sections.

5. Results for each query. (A memo to your instructor discussing these results should also be provided.)

6. As mentioned above, you should prepare an oral presentation. (Your instructor will establish the time allocated to your presentation.) You should use a presentation package and discuss the key features of your database. Also, discuss how this database is beneficial for Ms. Hannah. What additional data could be stored in the database?

CASE

11

Friends In Need

Database Case　　　　　**Difficulty Rating:** ★

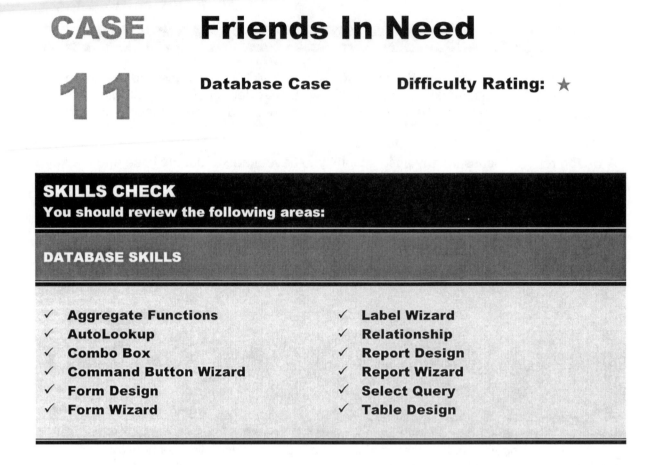

SKILLS CHECK
You should review the following areas:

DATABASE SKILLS

- ✓ Aggregate Functions
- ✓ AutoLookup
- ✓ Combo Box
- ✓ Command Button Wizard
- ✓ Form Design
- ✓ Form Wizard

- ✓ Label Wizard
- ✓ Relationship
- ✓ Report Design
- ✓ Report Wizard
- ✓ Select Query
- ✓ Table Design

CASE BACKGROUND

Friends In Need is a well-respected charitable organization, often mentioned in the press for providing outstanding charitable services to local families. Currently, Friends In Need has a staff of 10 volunteers, including Roman Kieffer, who serves as the organization's director. Since the charitable organization's founding five years ago, the number and type of donations has continued to increase, necessitating changes in the way donations are currently tracked and distributed.

While the donation and distribution processes are simple in concept, paperwork is mounting. Currently, Mr. Kieffer keeps the charity's records in spiral notebooks, and he needs a better method for tracking donors and distributing donations to qualifying families. Recently the Byrd Corporation donated the necessary hardware and software needed to create a computerized information system for Friends In Need. Mr. Kieffer asks you to organize and automate the charity's record keeping activities. You will build and populate Donor, Donation, and Type tables; create New Donor and New Donation forms; prepare mailing labels and a Weekly Donations report; create relationships; and construct several queries.

CASE SCENARIO

One evening five years ago, Roman Kieffer watched a news program that discussed how several local families were having difficult times and unable to give their children Christmas presents. In an effort to help these families, Roman and several friends organized a charity drive, collecting toys, clothing, monetary gifts, and food items. The donations were then distributed to deserving families. The charity drive was so successful that Roman founded the Friends In Need charitable organization.

Since the charity's founding five years ago, the donation process has remained simple. When a donor makes a contribution, he either mails a check or drops by the Friends In Need Center. When a donation is made, a staff member records the donor's name, address, and phone number on a donation form, along with details about the donation. A receipt is then given to the donor. If the donor wishes to remain anonymous, the word "anonymous" is written across the donation form. Monetary donations are deposited in a local bank, while nonmonetary donations are sorted according to type. Each week, the Friends In Need committee evaluates assistance requests. Donations are then distributed to qualifying families, based on type of need.

Currently, all record keeping is tedious, inefficient, time-consuming, and manually performed. The manual, paper-based system is no longer adequate. As the newest Friends In Need volunteer, Roman asks you to build the Friends database. In order to construct the Friends database to Roman's specifications, you will build and populate Donor, Donation, and Type tables; design New Donor and New Donation forms; prepare mailing labels and a Weekly Donations report; create several relationships; and construct several queries.

Storage Specifications

After meeting with Mr. Kieffer and reviewing the forms and reports currently used by the charity, you decide the Friends database should have three tables: Donor, Donation, and Type. (Your professor will provide you with the data to populate the Donor and Donation tables.) The Donor table stores the donor's identification number, type, first and last name, company name, address, and phone number. The DonorType field indicates whether or not the donor is a company or individual. When a company makes a donation, the DonorType field is checked, indicating that the donor is a company. Information about the company's contact person is then entered into the LastName and FirstName fields. If an individual makes a donation, the company name field is left blank, and all other fields are completed. The DonorID field serves as the primary key. Table 1 shows the structure for the Donor table.

The Donation table stores data about each donation. After studying your notes about the donation process, you decide the Donation table should use the structure shown in Table 2. Since a donor can make several donations on any given day, you decide to create a field called DonationID. This field serves as the primary key. For each donation, Roman wants to record the donation's approximate worth. You create an AppWorth field to hold this data.

Table 3 shows the structure for the Type table. The Type table stores type codes and brief descriptions about the kinds of donations accepted by the organization. Once the Type table is created, you use the data from Table 4 to populate the table.

Two relationships are necessary. First, you create a relationship between the Donor and Donation tables. Since the Donor and Donation tables have a DonorID field, you decide to use this common field to create a relationship between these two tables. Second, a relationship between the Donation and Type tables is required. As you study the Donation and Type tables, you notice that these tables both have a TCode field. You use this common field to create a relationship between the Donation and Type tables. For each relationship, you enforce referential integrity.

Table 1: Donor Table Structure

Field Name	Data Type	Field Description	Field Size	Comments
DonorID	AutoNumber	Is a unique number assigned to each donor. Serves as primary key.	Long Integer	Is required.
DonorType	Yes/No	Indicates whether the donor is a company or individual. "Yes" represents a company. Set the default value to "No".	Yes/No	Is required.
LastName	Text	Stores the donor's last name or the contact person's last name.	50	Is required.
FirstName	Text	Stores the donor's first name or the contact person's first name.	25	Is required.
CompanyName	Text	Stores the company's name.	50	
SAddress	Text	Stores the street address for the individual or company.	50	Is required.
City	Text	Stores the city for the individual or company. Set the default value to "Chicago".	25	Is required.
State	Text	Stores the state abbreviation for the individual or company. Set the default value to "IL".	2	Is required.
Zip	Text	Stores the zip code for the individual or company.	10	Is required.

Table 2: Donation Table Structure

Field Name	Data Type	Field Description	Field Size	Comments
DonationID	AutoNumber	Serves as the primary key.	Long Integer	Is required.
DonorID	Number	Is the donor identification number of the individual or company making the donation.	Long Integer	Is required.
DDate	Date/Time	Stores the date the donation was made. Use Short Date as the format.		Is required.
TCode	Text	Stores the donation type code.	4	
AppWorth	Currency	Stores the approximate worth of the donation. Use a standard format.		
Comments	Memo	Stores comments about the donation.		

Table 3: Type Table Structure

Field Name	Data Type	Field Description	Field Size	Comments
TCode	Text	Serves as the primary key.	4	Is required.
TDescription	Text	Provides a brief description of the type.	25	Is required.

Table 4: Type Table Records

TCode	TDescription
T1	Monetary
T2	Food
T3	Clothing
T4	Toys
T5	Other

Input Specifications

When a new donor makes a contribution, the New Donor form captures contact information; this information is then stored in the Donor table. The contact information enables the charity to contact the donor about upcoming events and send out thank you letters for current and future donations. Figure 1 shows a sketch of the New Donor form. As you examine the sketch, you decide to use the Form Wizard to create an initial form. Once the initial form is created, you modify the form's appearance in Design view. To enhance the form's appearance, you decide to include graphics on the form.

Roman wants information about each donation captured and stored in the database. The New Donation form captures the donor's identification number, donation date, donation type, the donation's approximate worth, and comments. Roman wants to select a donor's identification number from a Combo box and then have the system look up the donor's first and last name. He also wants to select the donation type from a Combo box. Since a donor can make more than one donation at a time, you decide to include a command button on the form. This button, when pressed, allows a staff member to add information about a new donation, thus facilitating data entry. Figure 2 shows a tentative sketch of the New Donation form. Since this form uses data from multiple tables, you decide to first create a select query. You use the Form Wizard to create an initial New Donation form based on the query and then edit the form in Design view. You decide that this form should also include graphics.

Mr. Kieffer mentions that you are free to modify each form's design. However, the design must have a professional appearance, be consistent, and capture, at a minimum, the data as shown.

Figure 1: New Donor Form

Friends In Need

New Donor

Donor Identification Number: Last Name: First Name:

Donor Type:

Company Name: Street Address:

City: State: Zip:

Figure 2: New Donation Form

Friends In Need
New Donation
(Donation Date)

Donor Identification Number: Donor Name: Donation Type:

                                                                     Approximate Worth:

Comments:

Include a command button ──────▶   Add Donation

Information Specifications

Each Monday, Roman sends thank you letters to the individuals and companies who made donations the previous week. Since donor addresses are now stored in the database, you decide to generate mailing labels for him. You prepare a select query that retrieves contact information for the previous week's donors and sorts the donor last names in ascending order. You then use the Report Wizard to prepare mailing labels. Figure 3 shows a sketch of the mailing labels. (The actual data for the mailing labels may differ from what is shown below.)

Roman wants a report showing the types of donations that were made last week and their approximate values. Figure 4 shows a tentative sketch of the Weekly Donations report. The report header includes the report title, the current date, and graphics. The report body shows the donation types, donor identification numbers, and the approximate worth of the donations. Roman wants this information sorted in ascending order by donation type. Within the donor type category, he wants the information sorted in ascending order based on the donor identification number. Since this report requires data from multiple tables, you build a select query, and then base the report on the query.

Figure 3: Mailing Labels

Jwang Buyung
5010 Jackson Drive
Chicago, IL 60611

Woody Huang
777 Kelley Avenue
Chicago, IL 60612

Rayna Reyes
1801 Sandhurst
Chicago, IL 60601

Johnny Richards
1020 Beagle Drive
Chicago, IL 60612

Catrina Stanton
Betty's Interior Designs
4651 Asheville Lane
Chicago, IL 60613

Figure 4: Weekly Donations Report

Friends In Need
Weekly Donations
(Current Date)

Donation Type	Donor ID	Approximate Worth
Clothing	2	$30.00
	5	$15.00
	13	$5.00
	.	
	.	
	.	
Food	3	$50.00
	12	$10.00
	.	
	.	
	.	

Mr. Kieffer requires answers for the following questions. Build queries to help Mr. Kieffer answer these questions. If you choose, you may generate reports based on these queries.

1. Which donation type is most popular? Mr. Kieffer wants a count for each donation type. Show only the type descriptions (TDescription) and their counts. No other fields should be shown.

2. How many companies made donations last week? (Use February 16, 2003 as the beginning date for the previous week.)

3. Which of the charity's donors made contributions worth more than $500.00? For each donor, show the first and last name, company name (if applicable), and approximate worth of the contribution.

4. Who are the contact persons for the companies that have contributed to the charity? Show the company name and then the first and last name of the contact person. Sort the information in ascending order based on company name.

5. On average, what is the approximate worth of the donations made last week? (Use February 16, 2003 as the beginning date for the previous week.)

Implementation Concerns

For this case, you design and populate Donor, Donation, and Type tables; design New Donor and New Donation forms; prepare mailing labels and a Weekly Donations report; create several queries; and establish relationships between tables.

As mentioned in the Storage Specification section, you create relationships between the Donor and Donation tables and the Donation and Type tables. For each relationship, you should enforce referential integrity.

As previously mentioned, New Donor and New Donation forms are necessary. A simple way to create the New Donor form is to use the Form Wizard. Once you have created an initial form, edit the form in Design view. Several options are available for creating the New Donation Form. One option is to create a select query and then use the Form Wizard to create an initial form. Once the form is created, the form's appearance can be edited in Design view. The New Donation form in Figure 2 includes an Add Donation button. The Command Button Wizard enables you to easily include this record operation feature.

Since thank you letters are sent to donors for the previous week, you need a select query to identify these donors. Once the donors are identified, you can use the Label Wizard to create mailing labels. For the Weekly Donations report, you should construct a select query to retrieve the necessary data, and then use the Report Wizard to create the report.

Test Your Design

After creating the forms, tables, relationships, queries, and reports, you should test your database design. Perform the following transactions:

1. The charity has several new donors. Enter their contact information and contributions into the database.
   - Bobak Nazar donated $450.00 on February 19, 2003. His contact information is 1220 Hemingway Drive, Chicago, IL 60661. Also, enter the following comment: "A check for $247 was provided, along with $203 in cash."
   - Kwai Chang donated approximately $100 in food items on February 19, 2003. His contact information is 17493 Kelley Drive, Chicago, IL 60664.
   - Carmelo Pereles donated approximately $250 in baby clothes on February 20, 2003. Her contact information is 3321 Beverly Drive, Chicago, IL 60667. Also, enter the following comment: "The clothes range in size from newborn to toddler."

2. Enter the following contributions for existing donors into the Friends database:
   - On behalf of Lancaster Paints, Robin Bibb donated $5,000 in cash, $3,000 in food items and $2,500 in clothing to the charity on February 20, 2003.
   - On behalf of Betty's Interior Designs, Catrina Stanton donated $1,557.74 in cash, $750.00 in toys, and $32.30 in clothing to the charity on February 21, 2003. Also, enter the following comment: "The toys are most appropriate for children over the age of three."

CASE DELIVERABLES

In order to satisfactorily complete this case, you should build the database and then prepare both written and oral presentations. Unless otherwise specified, submit the following deliverables to your professor. Also, unless otherwise specified, perform these steps after you have tested your design.

1. A written report discussing any assumptions you have made about the case and the key elements of the case. Additionally, what features did you add to make the database more functional? User friendly? (Please note that these assumptions cannot violate any of the requirements specified above and must be approved by your professor.)

2. A printout of each form.

3. A printout of each report. (Where applicable, use the week of February 16, 2003 as the beginning date for previous week.)

4. An electronic, working copy of your database that meets the criteria mentioned in the case scenario and specifications sections.

5. Results for each query. (A memo to your instructor discussing these results should also be provided.)

6. As mentioned above, you should prepare an oral presentation. (Your instructor will establish the time allocated to your presentation.) You should use a presentation package and discuss the key features of your database. Also, discuss how this database is beneficial for Roman. What changes to this database would you recommend? What additional data could be stored in the database?

CASE 12 Susan's Special Sauces

Database Case   **Difficulty Rating:** ★★

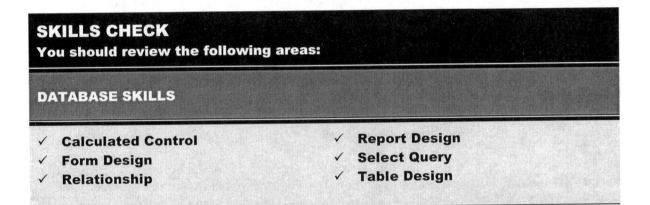

SKILLS CHECK
You should review the following areas:

DATABASE SKILLS

- ✓ Calculated Control
- ✓ Form Design
- ✓ Relationship

- ✓ Report Design
- ✓ Select Query
- ✓ Table Design

CASE BACKGROUND

Susan's Special Sauces is a small company that produces a variety of salad dressings and sauces. Joy Giovanni, the company's owner, recently purchased a building on the outskirts of town and now wishes to become more organized with her record keeping, especially as it relates to inventory tracking. Initially, Joy wants you to build a database that allows her to monitor the inventory levels of the company's products. For instance, she would like to know current inventory levels, maximum inventory levels, minimum inventory levels, production costs, and selling prices for the company's products. She needs simple, effective forms for entering data about her products. She needs reports that identify low-in-stock items and items that are currently in inventory. She also needs to extract specific information about the company's products and product categories from the database.

CASE SCENARIO

Joy Giovanni owns and operates a small, Texas-based company called Susan's Special Sauces. Joy named the company after her grandmother and one of her daughters. Susan's Special Sauces produces and sells a variety of salad dressings and sauces, ranging from Creamy Italian Salad Dressing to Extra Spicy Barbecue Sauce. In the early years of her business, Joy prepared, packaged and sold a variety of spaghetti sauces at local and state fairs, conventions and flea markets. Over the years, Joy increased her company's product offerings to include gourmet salad dressings, pasta sauces, barbecue sauces, and steak sauces. Susan's Special Sauces currently offers 20 products in five product categories. Table 1 shows the company's current product list.

Randolph Restaurants, a small restaurant chain, uses and also sells many of the sauce company's products. In fact, Randolph Restaurants is the primary customer for Susan's Special Sauces. When the restaurant chain runs low on one of the sauce company's products, Mr. Randolph calls Joy and tells her which product he needs to replenish. The lead-time has been sufficient, so if Joy does not have the product already bottled, she prepares the product after the order is placed.

To date, Joy does not have a formalized method for tracking inventory. When Mr. Randolph calls, she writes the order down on any available scrap of paper or just relies on her memory. If she has the products already bottled, she boxes the order and then delivers the order to Mr. Randolph at one of his restaurants. If a new batch is required, Joy gives the order to her cooks. Sometimes, this method leads to problems with having too much or too little of a particular item on hand.

The growing popularity of the company's sauces has recently required the sauce company to move to a larger building. Customers can now purchase Susan's Special Sauces products from a small shop located in the front of the building.

Now that she has opened a shop, Joy recognizes the need to implement lead times and utilize safety stock. The lead-time to prepare new batches of dressings or special sauces is two days. In general, lead-time is the time it takes Joy to replenish her stock. To avoid stockouts, Joy also utilizes safety stock. Safety stock is extra bottles of the products that are kept on hand. Safety stock acts as a cushion, guarding against running out of a given product. Joy feels that each product's safety stock should be two days of expected daily demand.

Since Joy needs a more formalized method for tracking inventory, she asks you to build a simple inventory tracking system. During your first meeting with her, she mentions that she wants to track each product's selling price, quantity on hand and production cost. Additionally, the inventory tracking system should store the maximum and minimum inventory levels for each product. Joy provides you with a sheet, listing the maximum inventory levels for her products. However, she has not had time to determine the minimum inventory levels for all of her products. She asks you to determine the minimum inventory levels for each product and then insert this information into the database. (A formula is provided in the next section.) Initially, you will build the portion of the database that provides Joy with this information.

Storage Specifications

As you review your notes from your meeting with Joy, you realize that Product and Category tables are needed. The Product table contains nine fields, and its structure is shown in Table 2. (Once you have created the table, use the records provided in Table 1 to populate the table.) As you are constructing the Product table, you recall that Joy asked you to determine each product's minimum inventory level. After you determine each product's minimum inventory level, you create the MinInvLev field for the Product table, and then insert the minimum inventory level data into this field. During your meeting with Joy, she recommended that you use the following formula for calculating a product's minimum inventory level.

Minimum Inventory Level = (Demand During Lead Time + Safety Stock).

Since the Category table contains four fields, it is easy to construct. Table 3 shows the Category table's structure, and Table 4 contains the records for the Category table.

Since Joy has requested information that requires data from two tables, you establish a relationship between the Product and Category tables. Since each table contains a PFamilyCode field, you use this common field to join the two tables.

Table 1: Product Records

Product No	Product Name	Product Family Code	Quantity On Hand	Selling Price	Production Cost	Expected Daily Demand	Maximum Inventory Level
1	Extra Creamy Ranch Dressing	DR	140	$3.50	$2.00	25	150
2	Extra Creamy Italian Dressing	DR	100	$3.50	$2.00	35	210
3	Italian Dressing	DR	100	$3.00	$1.50	40	240
4	Superior Caesar Salad Dressing	DR	150	$3.25	$1.25	40	240
5	Susan's French Dressing	DR	119	$3.25	$1.25	42	252
6	Susan's Thousand Island Dressing	DR	125	$3.25	$1.25	55	330
7	Susan's Creamy Blue Cheese Dressing	DR	330	$3.25	$1.25	55	330
8	Sensational Steak Sauce	SA	202	$4.50	$2.50	45	270
9	Thick and Hearty Sensational Steak Sauce	SA	40	$4.75	$2.75	30	180
10	Meatball Express	PS	180	$4.35	$2.85	30	180
11	Vegetarian's Delight	PS	150	$4.50	$2.90	30	180
12	Garlic, Onion and Mushrooms	PS	30	$4.50	$3.00	5	30
13	More Cheese, Please	PS	4	$4.75	$3.50	15	90
14	Mild Picante	SL	149	$3.10	$1.55	25	150
15	Medium Picante	SL	130	$3.10	$1.55	25	150
16	Jumpin' Hot Picante	SL	115	$3.10	$1.55	20	120
17	Hickory Smoke Barbecue Sauce	BS	130	$4.90	$2.95	25	150
18	Uncle Steve's Best Ever Barbecue Sauce	BS	164	$5.90	$3.45	30	180
19	Magnificent Mesquite Flavored Barbecue Sauce	BS	110	$4.75	$2.75	20	120
20	Extra Spicy Barbecue Sauce	BS	101	$4.50	$2.25	25	150

CASE 12: Susan's Special Sauces

Table 2: Product Table Structure

Field Name	Data Type	Field Description	Field Size	Comments
PNo	Number	Serves as the primary key. Is unique.	Long Integer	Is required.
PName	Text	Identifies the product.	45	Is required.
PFamilyCode	Text	Identifies the category to which the product belongs.	4	Is required.
QOH	Number	Identifies the number of units currently on hand.	Long Integer	Is required.
SellingPrice	Currency	Identifies the selling price of the product.	Currency	Is required.
PCost	Currency	Identifies how much it costs us per unit to produce this product.	Currency	Is required.
MinInvLev	Number	Identifies the amount we should keep on hand. New batches are made when we reach this level.	Long Integer	
DailyDemand	Number	Identifies the average daily demand.	Long Integer	
MaxInvLev	Number	Identifies the maximum level of inventory.	Long Integer	

Table 3: Category Table Structure

Field Name	Data Type	Field Description	Field Size	Comments
PFamilyCode	Text	Is a unique number. Use as the primary key.	4	Is required.
Description	Text	Contains the product family name.	15	Is required.
NoInFamily	Number	Contains the number of products in this category.	Long Integer	
Comments	Memo	Contains comments about this category.		

80

Table 4: Category Records

PFamilyCode	Description	NoInFamily
BS	Barbecue Sauce	4
DR	Dressing	7
PS	Pasta Sauce	4
SA	Steak Sauce	2
SL	Salsa	3

Input Specifications

You prepare sketches of the Product and Category forms and schedule a meeting with Joy. Figures 1 and 2 show these sketches. During the meeting, Joy expresses her delight with the sketches; however, she encourages you to be creative with the design. She also requests that the forms use a consistent format, be user friendly, include the business name, and have a picture of a sauce bottle in the header. (You will need to locate a picture to include on each form.)

After your meeting with Joy, you begin working on the forms. As you study the sketch for the Product form, you decide the main purpose of the form is to enable Joy to add, modify or delete products from the database. You also decide the form should include all fields from the Product table. As you study the Category form sketch, you recognize the simplicity of this form. This form contains only four fields and is used by Joy to add, modify and delete information about each product family category.

Figure 1: Product Form

Susan's Special Sauces

Product Form

Product No:

Product Name:

Product Family Code:

Selling Price:
Production Cost:

Quantity On Hand:

Expected Daily Demand:

Minimum Inventory Level:
Maximum Inventory Level:

Figure 2: Category Form

Susan's Special Sauces
Category Form

Family Code: Description:

Products In Family: Comments:

Information Specifications

Joy needs a Weekly Inventory Report and Low-In-Stock Report. She has developed sketches for these reports. Figures 3 and 4 show these preliminary sketches. As Joy hands you the sketches, she mentions that you are free to modify each report's overall appearance; however, each report should provide the required information and have a professional appearance.

The Weekly Inventory Report is prepared each Friday afternoon and provides Joy with detailed information about each product. She would like the Weekly Inventory Report format to resemble Figure 3. The report header includes the report's title and current date. Joy wants the Weekly Inventory Report to group the products by product category. The product categories should be sorted in ascending order. Joy would like the products within each category sorted in ascending order. For each product, Joy wants to see the product's name, number, quantity on hand, minimum inventory level, and current selling price. Use the column headings shown in Figure 3. Since this is a multi-page report, Joy wants the column headings to appear on each page. She also would like a page number to appear in each page's footer. She also wants each report field to be formatted appropriately. For instance, make sure the current selling price uses a currency format. Joy would like the product category headings to stand out, so she requests that you bold these headings on the report. Keep in mind that this report is based on a select query, and the query uses data from the Product and Category tables.

Joy wants the Low-In-Stock Report to identify all products whose current quantity on hand is equal to or below the minimum inventory level. If a product's quantity on hand is equal to or below the minimum inventory level, Joy will then request that the recommended batch amount be produced to replenish each low-in-stock product. The Recommended Batch Amount is determined by subtracting the Quantity on Hand from the Maximum Inventory Level.

Figure 4 shows a sketch of the Low-In-Stock Report. As you review the sketch, you notice that the report header displays the report's title and current date. Joy has said that this report must contain product name, number, quantity on hand, minimum inventory level, and recommended batch amount columns. Joy wants the products listed in ascending order. In order to build this report, you decide to construct a select query based on the Product table and then base the report on the select query. To enhance the report, you place a page number in the page footer.

Figure 3: Weekly Inventory Report

Susan's Special Sauces

Weekly Inventory Report
(Current Date)

Product Name	Product Number	Quantity On Hand	Minimum Inventory Level	Current Selling Price
Barbecue Sauce				
Extra Spicy Barbecue Sauce				
Hickory Smoke Barbecue Sauce				
.				
.				
.				
Dressing				
Extra Creamy Italian Dressing				
Italian Dressing				
.				
.				
.				

Figure 4: Low-In-Stock Report

Susan's Special Sauces

Low-In-Stock Report
(Current Date)

Product Name	Product Number	Quantity On Hand	Minimum Inventory Level	Recommended Batch Amount
Extra Spicy Barbecue Sauce				
Hickory Smoke Barbecue Sauce				
.				
.				
.				

Joy needs answers for the following questions. Build queries to help Joy answer these questions. If you choose, you may generate reports based on these queries.

1. Which products have a unit profit margin less than $2.00? For each product, include the product's name, number and unit profit margin. (No other fields should be included.)

2. Which products have a unit profit margin equal to or greater than $2.00? For each product, include the product's name, number and unit profit margin. (No other fields should be included.)

3. Which products cost Joy less than $2.50 per unit to produce? For each product, include the product's name, number and production cost. (No other fields should be included.)

4. Which products cost Joy more than $3.00 per unit to produce? For each product, include the product's name, number and production cost. (No other fields should be included.)

5. Which products have a minimum inventory level greater than 150? For each product, include the product's name and minimum inventory level. (No other fields should be included.)

Implementation Concerns

In order to build the inventory tracking system described in the case scenario, you will build two tables, two forms, two reports, and several select queries. You will also establish a relationship between the Product and Category tables. The forms require you to insert a picture. You will need to locate a picture to insert. Several of the select queries require you to sort, specify criteria, create expressions, and use data from two tables. In order to design the reports, you will base the reports on queries, specify sort orders and work with report headers, footers, and page headers.

Test Your Design

After creating the tables, forms, queries, relationships, and reports, you should test your database design. Perform the following transactions.

1. Joy wishes to add a new product category to the database. The new product family is cocktail sauce; the product family code is CS, and the number of products currently in the family is 1.

2. Joy has developed several new products and wishes to offer them for sale. Enter the following products into the database.

Product No	Product Name	Product Family Code	Quantity On Hand	Selling Price	Production Cost	Expected Daily Demand	Maximum Inventory Level
21	Lite Italian Dressing	DR	100	$3.50	$2.00	25	150
22	Lite Superior Caesar Salad Dressing	DR	100	$3.50	$2.00	5	30
23	Traditional Meat Spaghetti Sauce	PS	150	$5.00	$3.50	25	150
24	Southern Barbecue Sauce	BS	150	$5.00	$3.00	25	150
25	Grandma's Cocktail Sauce	CS	150	$2.00	$.75	15	90

3. Joy no longer wishes to sell the Garlic, Onion and Mushrooms pasta sauce. Delete this product from the Product table.

4. The daily demand for the Superior Caesar Salad Dressing has increased to 75 units. Update your database to reflect this change.

5. Identify the five products that have the highest expected daily demand. List only the product name and expected daily demand fields.

CASE DELIVERABLES

In order to satisfactorily complete this case, you should build the database and then prepare both written and oral presentations. Unless otherwise specified, submit the following deliverables to your professor. Also, unless otherwise specified, perform the following steps after you test your design.

1. A written report discussing any assumptions you have made about the case and the key elements of the case. Additionally, what features did you add to make the database more functional? User friendly? (Please note that these assumptions cannot violate any of the requirements specified above and must be approved by your professor.)

2. A printout of each form.

3. A printout of each report.

4. An electronic, working copy of your database that meets the criteria mentioned in the case scenario and specifications sections.

5. Results for each query. (A memo to your instructor discussing these results should also be provided.)

6. As mentioned above, you should prepare an oral presentation. (Your instructor will establish the time allocated to your presentation.) You should use a presentation package and discuss the key features of your database. Also, discuss how this database is beneficial for Joy.

CASE

13

Second Time Around Movies

Database Case **Difficulty Rating:** ★★

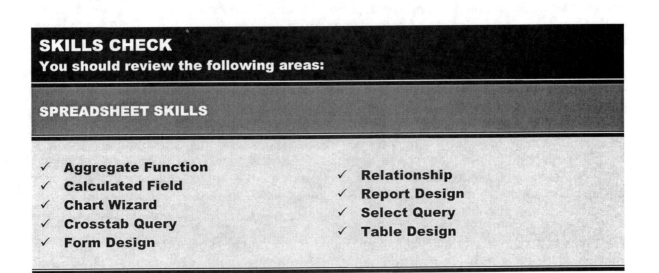

CASE BACKGROUND

Sharrie Daniels owns and operates a local chain of video rental stores. Although business is steady, competition is forcing her to find new, innovative ways to market her business. Taylor and Berkley Daniels, having inherited their grandmother's entrepreneurial spirit, recognize the significance of using the Web to strengthen the family business. Last year the twins approached their grandmother about creating an online movie rental business. Although the new business's primary target market is the avid Web surfer, the twins think the online movie rental business will prove popular with individuals seeking convenience or living in rural areas.

After initial test marketing, Sharrie gave the project a green light. With their grandmother's blessing and a significant advance on their inheritance, the twins opened Second Time Around Movies. Currently, Second Time Around Movies is doing well and serves five states: Arkansas, Kansas, Louisiana, Oklahoma, and Texas. If the business continues to do well, it will expand to other states.

The Second Time Around Movies database contains data about current movie club members, membership plans and the advertisement sources used to attract members. To make several marketing decisions, the twins need to extract and use data currently stored in this database. Taylor and Berkley are interested in learning more about their movie club members, investigating potential marketing opportunities and identifying the various advertisement sources that are currently attracting movie club members. The twins ask you to extract specific data and prepare several reports. As you examine the database, you realize that a Plans form and minor table modifications are also necessary.

CASE SCENARIO

Second Time Around Movies, the brainchild of Taylor and Berkley Daniels, is a new type of movie rental business. Rather than a traditional brick-and-mortar business, Second Time Around Movies is an online movie rental store. Second Time Around Movies offers its movie club members a wide selection of both new releases and classic movies on DVDs. In fact, Second Time Around Movies has over 9,000 titles available for rental.

Second Time Around Movies offers its movie club members the convenience of renting movies from the comfort of their homes. Movie club members rent DVDs online, saving the time and expense of running to the local video store to check out or return videos.

To take advantage of the online movie store, a Web site visitor must subscribe and pay a monthly membership fee. The monthly membership fee is based on the size of the movie package. Until the membership subscription is cancelled, the movie club member's credit card is billed a monthly membership fee. A member is free to change or cancel his membership plan at anytime.

The online subscription form collects basic customer information, including credit card number, shipping address, e-mail address, and monthly newspaper request. At the time of enrollment, a subscriber selects a membership plan that is suitable to his viewing needs. During the subscription process, a new member indicates whether or not he would like to receive the Second Time Around Movies newspaper. This newspaper provides movie reviews, offers promotions, identifies upcoming releases, and is a good way for the twins to keep in touch with current movie club members.

Once a customer completes the subscription process and is approved, the customer builds his Movie Request List. A customer creates this list by selecting the movies he wishes to view. He will also rank these movies in order of viewing preference. The Movie Request List tells the Second Time Around Movies staff which movies the club member wishes to view or check out. Movie packages are then assembled based on the member's Movie Request List. Movie package refers to the number of DVDs shipped at one time to a movie club member.

While five plans are currently available, avid movie buffs can select the Seymour Movies plan, enabling them to receive as many as six DVDs at a time. In contrast, the occasional movie viewer may choose a more economical plan, such as the Blue Moon plan. The Blue Moon plan ships a single DVD at a time. Table 1 identifies the available membership plans, along with pricing for each plan.

Table 1: Available Membership Plans

PlanID	Description	Cost
001	Blue Moon	$12.99
002	Sharrie's Special	$17.99
003	Popcorn and More	$22.99
004	Couch Potato Special	$27.99
005	Seymour Movies	$34.99

At Second Time Around Movies, a current movie club member visits the company's Web site and adds movie names to his Movie Request List. If the movie is available, it is shipped as part of the member's next movie package. The number of DVDs contained within a movie package is determined by the selected membership plan. If a member is on the Just Released List, newly released movie DVDs are included as part of the next movie package being shipped to the customer.

Before receiving a new movie package, a club member must return all currently checked out DVDs. Returning DVDs is a simple process. After watching the DVDs, the customer places the DVDs in a specially marked, prepaid postage envelope and drops the envelope in the mail. When the Second Time Around Movies staff receives the envelope, a new movie package is mailed to the member. Usually, the member receives his new movie package within a few days.

Potential movie club members are discovering Second Time Around Movies in a variety of ways. Friends, television and print advertisements, other Web sites, and search engines are contributing to the new online store's success. Taylor and Berkley want to know how new movie club members learn about Second Time Around Movies. When subscribing, a new member is asked how he learned about the store. This information is then stored in the movie club member's record. Taylor and Berkley will use this information to better market their store in the future.

Taylor and Berkley want to modify the store's available membership plans. In order to do this, they need to know which plans are most popular. They also want to know how members are attracted to their online store. For instance, which advertisement source encouraged the member to visit the online store's Web site?

Since Taylor and Berkley are very busy managing the online movie rental store, they ask you to retrieve information from and make modifications to the Second Time Around Movies database. The following sections describe the information and the modifications that are needed.

Storage Specifications

Your database copy contains Member, Plan and Source tables. (Your instructor will provide you with a copy of the database. Your copy contains the tables and test data that you need for this case.) After examining the tables, you realize that a few modifications to the Member and Plan table structures are necessary. The Source table structure does not require modifications.

As you study the Member table, you notice that it contains a Newspaper field. This field indicates whether or not the member wishes to receive an electronic copy of the Second Time Around Movies monthly newspaper. You decide to set the Newspaper field's default value to "Yes" and use an input mask for the member's phone number.

Currently, the Plan table contains PlanID, Description and Cost fields. However, the Plan table is missing a MaxMovies field. When included, the MaxMovies field identifies the maximum number of movies available for check out according to a particular plan. You modify the Plan table to include this field. Table 2's fourth column contains the data that should be added to the Plan table.

Table 2: Plan Table

PlanID	Description	Cost	MaxMovies
001	Blue Moon	$12.99	1
002	Sharrie's Special	$17.99	2
003	Popcorn and More	$22.99	3
004	Couch Potato Special	$27.99	4
005	Seymour Movies	$34.99	6

Input Specifications

In the future, Taylor and Berkley will add, modify and delete several membership plans. To facilitate changes to the Plan table, you design a simple form that accommodates the addition, modification and deletion of membership plans. Taylor and Berkley provide you with a tentative sketch for the Membership Plan form. Figure 1 shows this tentative sketch. As you study the sketch, you realize that using a Form Wizard is an easy way to begin the form's development. As you continue to study the sketch, you decide that a picture is needed. Locate a picture and include this picture on the form. While you are free to work with the form's design, the form must contain, at a minimum, all fields from the Plan table, have a professional appearance and be easy to use.

Figure 1: Membership Plan Form

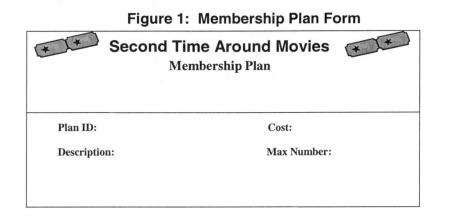

Information Specifications

Taylor and Berkley wonder which membership plan is the best seller. They also wonder how the plans compare with each other. Since charts provide a good way of summarizing and visually presenting information, you decide a pie chart will prove useful for comparing and contrasting the membership plans. You decide to use the Chart Wizard to construct a pie chart that summarizes the information requested by the twins. Figure 2 shows a representation of how this pie chart might look. (Your chart values will vary from the values shown in Figure 2. You may wish to use the system's online help feature to review chart creation.)

As you examine Figure 2, you notice that the report's title is "Membership Plan Comparison Chart" and a current date is included. Also, each pie slice represents one of the available membership plans, and a data label and percentage are shown above each pie slice. Taylor and Berkley are interested in examining the relationship between advertisement sources and states. Prepare a report similar to the one in Figure 3. Although you realize several methods for obtaining the report information exist, you construct a Crosstab query and base the Count By State report on this query. (Your counts will differ from the counts shown in Figure 3.)

The twins want to know which movie club members have requested a monthly newspaper. As mentioned previously, a new member specifies whether or not he wants to receive a monthly newspaper during the subscription process. Prepare a Newspaper Recipients report for the twins. Figure 4 provides a sketch of this report.

Figure 2: Membership Plan Comparison Chart

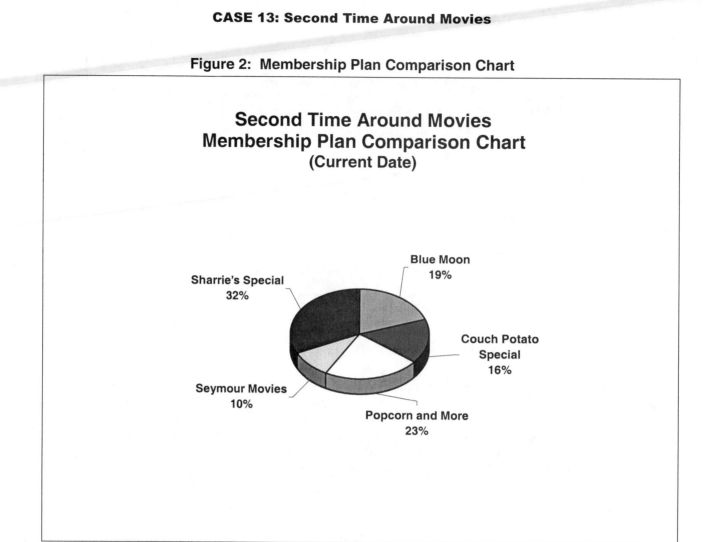

Second Time Around Movies
Membership Plan Comparison Chart
(Current Date)

Blue Moon
19%

Sharrie's Special
32%

Couch Potato
Special
16%

Seymour Movies
10%

Popcorn and More
23%

Figure 3: Count By State

Second Time Around Movies
Count By State
(Current Date)

Source Description	Arkansas	Kansas	Louisiana	Oklahoma	Texas	Count
Another Web Site	52	49	89	97	101	388
Friend						
Magazine						
.						
.						
.						

Total Count:

Figure 4: Newspaper Recipient Report

Second Time Around Movies
Newspaper Recipients
(Current Date)

Last Name	First Name	E-Mail Address
Kelly	Lisa	panda@excite.com
Kelly	Val	imafriend@hotmail.com
Lansing	Peter	plansing@home.com
.		
.		
.		

Taylor and Berkley need answers to the following questions. If you choose, you may generate reports based on these queries.

1. The twins want to approach one or two major credit card companies about possible promotional opportunities. Which credit cards are movie club members using? Which credit card company is used most frequently? (Your answer should identify the credit card company and indicate a member count by state for that credit card company.)

2. Which current members have Hotmail accounts? (Show the member's name, state and e-mail address.)

3. How many current members live in Texas towns? (Your results should list the town, a count for each town and an overall count.)

4. Taylor and Berkley want to know the total revenue generated by their membership plans for each Texas town. Your results should show the name of the Texas town and the total membership revenue for that town.

5. How did current movie club members from Kansas learn about the online movie store? (Show the results for the source description (not the source) and provide a count for each source description.

Implementation Concerns

This case requires you to modify tables, create a form, construct several queries, and prepare several reports. The table modification requires setting a default value for the Newspaper field and creating an input mask for the Phone Number field. To facilitate data entry to the Plans table, you will build a simple data entry form. This form will allow the twins to add, modify or delete membership plans. Since this is a simple form, you can use the AutoForm Wizard to build an initial form and then modify this form in design view.

To construct the Membership Plan Comparison Chart, which is a type of report, you should first build a select query to retrieve the necessary data. Keep in mind that this select query retrieves data from two tables and uses the Count function. Once you have created your select query, use the Chart Wizard to build your pie chart. The chart may require editing, so use the system's online help feature to learn more about editing charts. The chart should include the current date, have an appropriate header and be rotated to enhance its readability. Also, you should show a data label and percentage for each slice. Since the Newspaper Recipients report is based only on the Customer table, you can either create a select query and then use the Report Wizard or just use the Report Wizard to create this report. The Count By State report requires data from two tables. Construct a select query to retrieve the information, and then use the Report Wizard to build the report. Once the report is built, you can edit the design of the report.

Test Your Design

After making the requested changes specified in the case scenario, you should test your database design. Perform the following transactions.

1. Using your newly created Membership Plan form, change the price of each plan. Use the information provided in the following table.

PlanID	Description	Cost
001	Blue Moon	$14.99
002	Sharrie's Special	$18.99
003	Popcorn and More	$23.99
004	Couch Potato Special	$28.99
005	Seymour Movies	$36.99

2. The twins are interested in comparing the membership plans by state. Prepare plan comparison charts for both Texas and Louisiana. Your charts will be similar to the Plan Comparison Chart discussed previously and shown as a sketch in Figure 2.

CASE DELIVERABLES

In order to satisfactorily complete this case, you should make the requested table modifications and then build the form, queries and reports. You should also prepare both written and oral presentations. Unless otherwise specified, submit the following deliverables to your professor. Unless otherwise specified, perform these steps after you have tested your design.

1. A written report discussing any assumptions you have made about the case and the key elements of the case. Additionally, what features did you add to make the database more functional? User friendly? (Please note that these assumptions cannot violate any of the requirements specified above and must be approved by your professor.)

2. A printout of the form.

3. A printout of each report.

4. An electronic, working copy of your database that meets the criteria mentioned in the case scenario and specifications sections.

5. Results for each query. (A memo to your instructor discussing these results should also be provided.)

6. As mentioned above, you should prepare an oral presentation. (Your instructor will establish the time allocated to your presentation.) Instead of the queries and reports mentioned above, what other helpful information might the twins retrieve from the database? How could this information help them make better marketing decisions?

Keller Industries

- ✓ Aggregate Function
- ✓ AutoLookup Query
- ✓ Calculated Control
- ✓ Find Unmatched Query Wizard
- ✓ Form Design
- ✓ Lookup Wizard

- ✓ Parameter Query
- ✓ Relationship
- ✓ Report Design
- ✓ Select Query
- ✓ Table Design
- ✓ Update Query

CASE BACKGROUND

Keller Industries is a company with a growing problem. As more of its employees are issued personal computers, the management of these personal computers and the installed software on them is creating massive headaches for the IT Department. Since no formal hardware/software tracking system is currently utilized, the IT Department has no way of knowing what hardware is currently assigned to Keller Industries employees, nor does the IT staff know whether all of the installed software is licensed.

In an effort to better manage its hardware and software, Keller Industries has decided to formally track all hardware and software currently assigned to its employees. Initially, the system will track personal computer and software assignments. Mica Meyers, the IT Department Director, provides you with a copy of a partially completed Tracking database. She then asks you to build two forms and three reports, design and populate a Hardware table, establish relationships between tables, and construct several queries.

CASE SCENARIO

When a Keller Industries employee needs to upgrade his computer system, he simply calls the IT Department and makes a verbal request. An IT staff member prepares a work order, and if the work order is approved, the request is filled as soon as possible. After the work order is completed, the work order is filed in a filing cabinet, never to be seen again. The lack of a formal hardware/software tracking system creates headaches for the IT Department staff, since the staff has only a general idea about what hardware and software are currently used by Keller Industries employees. Also, many problems currently exist, such as theft, use of illegal software, and incompatibility.

No one can say for certain how many personal computers are owned by Keller Industries or guarantee that only licensed software is on the personal computers. To gain control of the situation, Ms. Meyers asks you to inventory all personal computers and available software. She asks you to assign a unique hardware identification number to each personal computer and then finish building the Tracking database. Initially, the Tracking database will track all available personal computers, software, and hardware/software assignments. (For simplicity, operating systems are not included as part of the software list.)

When a new personal computer is purchased, Ms. Meyers wants the details about the newly acquired personal computer entered into the Tracking database. An IT staff member uses a Hardware form to capture details about the computer, such as the hardware identification number, processor type, processor speed, RAM amount, model, manufacturer, hard drive capacity, and serial number. After the personal computer is assigned to an employee, an assignment field in the table stores the employee's identification number.

When a work order is completed, Ms. Meyers wants the information entered immediately into the Tracking database, making a Hardware/Software Assignment form necessary. This form allows the IT staff member to add, modify, or delete current hardware/software assignments.

Ms. Meyers knows the Tracking database contains important details about the hardware, software, and current hardware/software assignments. By generating reports based on this data, she can make valuable decisions. For instance, the Software Assignment report helps Ms. Meyers determine how many copies of a particular software title are currently installed. The Hardware report tells Ms. Meyers about the current hardware and software configurations used by Keller Industries employees. The Employee Assignment report shows the current hardware/software configurations for each employee. While the Hardware report organizes this information by computer, the Employee Assignment report arranges the information by employee, thus facilitating the review of information.

Storage Specifications

The Tracking database contains populated Software, Employee, and Config tables. As you study these tables, you notice that the Software table contains SID, Publisher, Title, and License fields. The SID field serves as the primary key, uniquely identifying a particular software package. The Publisher field identifies the company that publishes the software. The Title field includes the software package's name, and the License field indicates how many licenses the company has for that particular software package. The Employee table contains EID, Lname, and FName fields. The EID field stores the employee identification number and serves as the table's primary key. The LName and FName fields contain the employee's last name and first name, respectively. The Config table identifies the software that is currently stored on a particular computer. Currently, this table contains only two fields: HID and SID. The HID field identifies a particular computer, and the SID field identifies the software package. As you study this table, you realize that a particular computer can have more than one application program installed, so the HID and SID fields serve as a combination key.

Ms. Meyers gives you an electronic file containing data about each personal computer. As you study this file, you notice that the file contains data about the serial number, processor type, processor speed, RAM amount, hard drive capacity, model, and manufacturer for each computer. This file also contains an AssignedTo field, providing the identification number of the employee who is currently assigned the computer. You decide to use these fields for the Hardware table and design the table structure shown in Table 1. Once you build the Hardware table, you copy and paste the data from the electronic file into the Hardware table.

As you study your notes about the Tracking database, you realize at least three relationships are necessary and that these relationships should enforce referential integrity. First, you need a relationship between the Employee and Hardware tables. You join the tables on the EID field from the Employee table and the AssignedTo field from the Hardware table. Second, you need a relationship between the Hardware and Config tables. Since both tables have an HID field, you join the tables on this field. Third, you must establish a relationship between the Config and Software tables. Since both tables contain an SID field, you use the SID field to join the two tables.

Table 1: Hardware Table Structure

Field Name	Data Type	Field Description	Field Size	Comments
HID	Number	Stores the hardware identification number. Serves as primary key.	Integer	Is assigned by the IT staff and differs from the serial number. Is required.
PSpeed	Text	Identifies the processor's speed.	15	
PType	Text	Identifies the type of processor.	25	Is required.
SerialNo	Text	Identifies the computer's serial number and differs from the HID.	20	Is required.

HardDrive	Text	Identifies the hard drive capacity for this computer.	10	
RAM	Text	Identifies the amount of RAM currently installed on this computer.	10	
Manufacturer	Text	Contains the name of the company that manufactured the computer.	25	
Model	Text	Contains the model of the computer.	25	
Category	Text	Identifies the type (category) of computer.	10	
AssignedTo	Text	Stores the employee identification number for the employee who is currently assigned this computer.	4	

Input Specifications

Figures 1 and 2 provide sketches of the Hardware Entry and Hardware/Software Assignment forms. Although you are free to modify each form's design, the design must have a professional appearance and capture, at a minimum, the data as shown.

The IT staff needs a Hardware Entry form to capture data about newly purchased computers. Figure 1 shows a sketch of this form. Since the data captured by this form are stored in the Hardware table, you decide to use the Form Wizard to build this form. Once the form is created, you can modify its appearance in Design view.

The IT staff needs to know what software is installed on each personal computer. The Hardware/Software Assignment form enables the staff to add, modify and delete the software installation data for each personal computer. Figure 2 shows a sketch of this form.

When using the Hardware/Software Assignment form, Ms. Meyers wants the data entry process to be as simple as possible. For instance, Ms. Meyers wants to select an HID number from a Combo box and then have the system lookup the rest of the data shown in Figure 2, including any previously assigned software. You decide to use an AutoLookup query to automatically retrieve the data. When assigning software to a particular computer, Ms. Meyers wants to select an SID number, and then have the system lookup the title and publisher information. You realize that the AutoLookup query also facilitates the lookup process for the software data.

Figure 1: Hardware Entry Form

Hardware Entry

Hardware ID: **EID:**

Serial No: Manufacturer: RAM:

Category: Model: Hard Drive:

Processor Speed:

Processor Type:

Figure 2: Hardware/Software Assignment Form

Hardware/Software Assignment

Hardware ID: **EID:**

Serial No: Manufacturer: RAM:

Category: Model: Hard Drive:

Processor Speed:

Processor Type:

Software On This Computer:

SID	Title	Publisher

Information Specifications

Ms. Meyers requires three reports, including Software Assignment, Hardware, and Employee Assignment reports. These reports organize the data from the Tracking database in different ways, providing Ms. Meyers with different views of the data. Figures 3 - 5 show sketches of these reports. While Ms. Meyers encourages you to be creative with your report designs, she stresses that each report must provide the information shown in its sketch and have a professional appearance. She would like each report to have its name, current date, and a picture in the report header. Each report's page footer should contain a page number, as well as a count of the total number of pages in the report.

Ms. Meyers hands you a tentative sketch of the Software Assignment report. Figure 3 shows this sketch. As you examine the sketch, you notice that the Software Assignment report lists all currently licensed software packages, indicates on which machines the software packages are currently installed, and identifies the employees who are using the software packages. This report organizes the information alphabetically by software title. Within each software title category, the HIDs are sorted in ascending order. For each software title, a count of the number of installations is shown. Ms. Meyers uses this information to help verify that all software installations are licensed. You decide to build a select query to retrieve the data for this report, and then base the report on the select query.

Figure 4 shows a tentative sketch of the Hardware report. The Hardware report lists the company's personal computers in ascending order by HID. This report provides a description of each computer, listing the processor speed, processor type, RAM amount, and hard drive capacity. This report also shows what software is currently installed on the computer, as well as the employee who is assigned the computer.

Ms. Meyers wants to know what software and hardware are currently assigned to each Keller Industries employee. She would like this information organized by the employee's last name. Figure 5 shows a tentative sketch of the Employee Assignment report. As you study the sketch, you realize that an employee can have more than one computer assigned to him. You decide to perform a secondary sort based on the HID field.

Figure 3: Software Assignment Report

Software Title	Publisher	HID	Employee
IGRAFX Flowcharter	AEC Software	20	Dancer, Robin
			Number Installed:
Project 2000	Microsoft	1	Murphy, Agnes
			Number Installed:

Page X of XX

Figure 4: Hardware Report

Hardware
(Current Date)

HID	Hardware Description	Software	Employee
1	1 GHz Intel Celron 18MG 20GB	Office 2000 Professional Project 2000 Designer 6*i* Norton AntiVirus WordPerfect Office 2002	Murphy, Agnes
		. . .	
2	1.3 GHz Intel Celron 128MG 20GB	Office 2000 Professional	Vorse, Barry
		. . .	

Page X of XX

Figure 5: Employee Assignment Report

Employee Assignment
(Current Date)

Employee	HID	Hardware Description			Software
Murphy, Agnes					
	1	470023-294	1 GHz	Intel Celron	Office 2000 Professional Project 2000 Oracle Designer 6i Norton AntiVirus WordPerfect Office 2002
Vorse, Barry					
	2	470030-532	1.3 GHz	Intel Celron	Office 2000 Professional

Page X of XX

Ms. Meyers requires answers for the following questions. Build queries to help Ms. Meyers answer these questions. If you choose, you may generate reports based on these queries.

1. What software is not currently installed on any computer? Ms. Meyers wants only the software title. She does not wish to view any other fields.

2. Which Keller Industries employees have not been assigned a computer? Ms. Meyers would like to know the first and last names of these employees. She does not require any other information.

3. Which employees currently have Oracle Designer 6i installed on their computers? List only the first and last names of the employees. Sort this information in ascending order based on employee last name.

4. Three employees want a copy of Corel WordPerfect Office 2002 installed on their machines. How many copies of Corel WordPerfect Office 2002 are currently installed? Do we have enough licenses to accommodate these new requests?

5. Which employees have notebook computers? Provide the employee's first and last name, the manufacturer, model, processor type, and processor speed.

Implementation Concerns

To make the modifications required in the case scenario, you will design a table, build two forms, prepare three reports, establish relationships between tables, and construct several queries. Once you have created the Hardware table, the data for this table is stored in an electronic file. You can then copy and paste the data into the Hardware table.

When constructing the Hardware Entry form, consider using the Form Wizard. Once the basic form is created, you can easily make any necessary modifications to the form in Design view.

The Hardware/Software Assignment form is a main form with a subform. You should consider constructing an AutoLookup query and then use the Form Wizard to create the Hardware/Software Assignment form. Once you have created an initial form, you can edit the form in Design view.

Each report uses data from multiple tables. For each report, you should construct a query to retrieve the necessary information from the underlying tables and then base your report on the query. The Hardware/Software Assignment report provides a count for each software package currently installed on the company's personal computers. One method for obtaining the count is to use a calculated control in your report.

Test Your Design

After creating your table, forms, queries, relationships, and reports, you should test your database design. Perform the following transactions:

1. The IT Department recently purchased five new computers. Using the Hardware Entry form, enter the following information about each new computer into the Tracking database. The computers have not been assigned to an employee, so the AssignedTo field is not included in the table below.

HID	PSpeed	PType	SerialNo	HardDrive	Model	RAM	Manufacturer	Category
22	2.2 GHz	Intel Pentium 4	684922-12-4944	120 GB	700XL	1024 MB	Gateway	Desktop
23	2.2 GHz	Intel Pentium 4	483203-98-4935	40 GB	Evo Desktop	256 MB	Compaq	Desktop
24	2.2 GHz	Intel Pentium 4	483203-98-4935	40 GB	Evo Desktop	256 MB	Compaq	Desktop
25	2.2 GHz	Intel Pentium 4	444097-12-4944	120 GB	700XL	1024 MB	Gateway	Desktop
26	1.2 GHz	Intel Pentium 3	994847-90-0003	10 GB	Dell Inspiron	128 MB	Dell	Notebook

2. The IT Department made the following assignments.
   - Clint Zumwalt is assigned a personal computer; the HID is 22. He requests that copies of Microsoft Office 2000 Professional and Microsoft Project be installed.

- Marsha Leminsky is assigned a personal computer; the HID is 26. She requests that copies of Corel WordPerfect Office 2002, Norton AntiVirus, and SAS Statview 5.0 be installed.

3. Agnes Murphy no longer wants Microsoft Office 2002 and Oracle Designer 6i on her machine. Make the appropriate entries in the database.

4. How many Pentium 4 computers does the company currently have? How many of these machines are desktop computers? Notebooks?

5. How many Dell notebook computers does the company currently own?

6. How many computers do not have Norton AntiVirus software installed? Do you think all the computers should have the antivirus software installed? If so, make the necessary updates.

CASE DELIVERABLES

In order to satisfactorily complete this case, you should build the database and then prepare both written and oral presentations. Unless otherwise specified, submit the following deliverables to your professor.

1. A written report discussing any assumptions you have made about the case and the key elements of the case. Additionally, what features did you add to make the database more functional? User friendly? (Please note that these assumptions cannot violate any of the requirements specified above and must be approved by your professor.)

2. A printout of each form.

3. A printout of each report.

4. An electronic, working copy of your database that meets the criteria mentioned in the case scenario and specifications sections.

5. Results for each query. (A memo to your instructor discussing these results should also be provided.)

6. As mentioned above, you should prepare an oral presentation. (Your instructor will establish the time allocated to your presentation.) You should use a presentation package and discuss the key features of your database. Also, discuss how this database is beneficial for Ms. Meyers. What changes would you recommend?

ABC Inc.'s Health Benefits

15

Database Case   **Difficulty Rating:** ★★★

SKILLS CHECK
You should review the following areas:

DATABASE SKILLS

- ✓ Advanced Report Design
- ✓ Aggregate Function
- ✓ AutoLookup
- ✓ Calculated Control
- ✓ Filter By Form
- ✓ Form Design

- ✓ Form Wizard
- ✓ Lookup Wizard
- ✓ Relationship
- ✓ Select Query
- ✓ Subform
- ✓ Table Design

CASE BACKGROUND

When it comes to health care, ABC Inc. recognizes that its employees have different health care needs. The company utilizes a flexible benefits plan, allowing company employees to customize their health benefit plans based on personal preferences. The health benefits enrollment process begins in two months, and Mr. Antonio Gonzalez, the Human Resources Director, is anxious to update the company's Benefits database. Mr. Gonzalez has hired you to manage the updates to the Benefits database. In Monday's meeting with Mr. Gonzalez, you were given a list of specifications for the database. These specifications require you to build an Employee Insurance Enrollment form, build and populate Employee and Select tables, construct several queries, prepare an Employees by Insurance report, and prepare a Personalized Employee Enrollment report for each ABC Inc. employee.

CASE SCENARIO

ABC Inc.'s Human Resources Department utilizes a "cafeteria-style" approach to providing its employees with health care benefits. Each fall, ABC Inc. employees review their current benefits, modify their elections, and then sign Section 125 forms. These changes must be entered into the Benefits database.

For medical insurance, an employee enrolls with a preferred provider organization (PPO) or a health maintenance organization (HMO). ABC Inc. currently pays the monthly medical premiums for its employees. However, if an employee enrolls in a dental plan or vision plan, the employee pays a modest monthly premium for the optional plan. An employee may carry medical, dental, and/or vision coverage for one or more of his family members. In order to carry insurance on a family member, the employee must carry the same coverage. For instance, to carry dental insurance on a spouse, the employee must also carry dental insurance on himself.

In a few weeks, an enrollment letter and an ABC Rates Change Schedule will be mailed to each employee. The enrollment letter notifies the employee about the upcoming enrollment period, providing time and location information. The ABC Rates Change Schedule lists the new health benefit rates, effective January 1. Table 1 shows the new ABC Rates Change Schedule.

After reviewing your notes from your meeting with Mr. Gonzalez, you realize that several modifications to the current Benefits database are necessary. These modifications require you to build an Employee Insurance Enrollment form, build and populate Employee and Select tables, construct several queries, prepare an Employees by Insurance report, and prepare a Personalized Employee Enrollment report for each ABC Inc. employee.

Table 1: ABC Rates Change Schedule
(Effective January 1st)

Insurance Company	Rates					
	E	S	S1	S2	C1	C2
All American Life Care (AALC)–PPO	$00.00	$281.22	$462.06	$523.54	$180.84	$242.32
Best Health Care (BHC)–HMO	$00.00	$263.07	$405.64	$455.54	$142.57	$192.47
Midwest Dental (MD)	$15.89	$37.92	$67.96	$78.29	$30.04	$40.37
Perfect Vision (PV)	$18.44	$25.78	$48.64	$79.27	$22.86	$30.63

E = Employee Only
S = Spouse Only
S1 = Spouse and Only One Child

S2 = Spouse and Two or More Children
C1 = Only One Child
C2 = Two or More Children

Storage Specifications

The Benefits database includes populated Company, Dependent, and Rate tables. As you study these tables, you notice that the Company table currently contains information about each insurance company. For each insurance company, an insurance company code (InsCode), company name (InsName), and brief description (Comments) are stored. The Dependent table identifies the dependent codes (DepCode) and provides descriptions of these codes (DepDesc). The Rate table contains InsCode, DepCode, and Rate fields. The Rate table has a combination key, consisting of the InsCode and DepCode fields. The Rate table contains current insurance rate information and will be updated to reflect the changes outlined in Table 1.

During a meeting with Mr. Gonzalez, he gives you an electronic file containing the data that you need to populate the Employee and Select tables. After meeting with Mr. Gonzalez, you decide to use the structures shown in Tables 2 and 3 for the Employee and Select tables. For the Employee table, you decide that the EID field should serve as the primary key, and the State field should use a default value of "TX". You then build the Employee table.

As you study the Select table's design, you determine that the table's primary key is a combination key, consisting of the EID, DepCode, and InsCode fields. The EffectiveDate field contains the date the policy takes effect. While this date is usually January 1, it can differ. For instance, an employee hired in the middle of the year will have a different effective date. You realize that the data values for the EID, DepCode, and InsCode fields are already stored in the Employee, Dependent, and Company tables, respectively. To facilitate data entry, you decide to use the Lookup Wizard to create a list of values for these fields.

The Lookup Wizard creates relationships between the Select table and the Employee, Company, and Dependent tables. You also decide these relationships should enforce referential integrity. You edit each relationship's join properties to enforce referential integrity.

Table 2: Employee Table Structure

Field Name	Data Type	Field Description	Field Size	Comments
EID	Number	Stores the employee's identification number. This number is unique. Serves as primary key.	Long Integer	Set the format property to 00000. This field is required.
DeptID	Number	Stores the department code. This number is unique.	Long Integer	Set the format property to 00. This field is required.
EFirstName	Text	Stores the employee's first name.	50	
ELastName	Text	Stores the employee's last name.	50	
StreetAddress	Text	Stores the employee's street address.	50	
City	Text	Stores the city where the employee lives.	50	
State	Text	Stores the state where the employee lives.	9	The state abbreviation should display in all caps. The default value is "TX".
ZipCode	Text	Stores the employee's zip code.	10	Use an input mask.
OfficeExt	Text	Stores the employee's office extension number.	4	

Table 3: Select Table Structure

Field Name	Data Type	Field Description	Field Size	Comments
EID	Number	Contains the employee's identification number. Serves as part of the combination key.	Long Integer	Set the format property to 00000. This field is required. This number is located in the Employee table.
DepCode	Text	Stores the dependent code. Serves as part of the combination key.	3	This code is taken from the Dependent table.
InsCode	Text	Stores the insurance company's code. Serves as part of the combination key.	4	This code is taken from the Insurance table.
EffectiveDate	Date/Time	Stores the date the policy becomes effective.	Short Date	

Input Specifications

The Benefits database requires an Employee Insurance Enrollment form. Figure 1 shows a tentative sketch of this form. Since the Employee Insurance Enrollment form uses data from three tables, you decide to construct a select query. Once you create the select query, you can use the Form Wizard to expedite the creation of the Employee Insurance Enrollment form. (You may wish to view your system's online help feature to review the Form Wizard and subforms.)

As you study the Employee Insurance Enrollment form sketch, you note that the Monthly Payroll Deduction field displays the sum of the employee's monthly health insurance premiums. You need an expression to calculate the value for this field. A quick search of the system's online help feature provides you with the following expression. You modify this expression to use your form and field names.

=Forms![Main Form Name]![Subform Name]![Field Name]

Figure 1: Employee Insurance Enrollment Form

ABC	**Employee Insurance Enrollment**	ABC

Employee ID: 00005

Employee Name: Votaw, Jaque
Employee Address: 203 Chowning Avenue
                          Arlington, TX 76004

Monthly Payroll Deduction: $379.25

Enrollment Options:

Dependent Code	Insurance Code	Rate	Effective Date
S	AALC	$281.22	1/1/2003
S	PV	$25.78	1/1/2003
S	MD	$37.92	1/1/2003
E	PV	$15.89	1/1/2003
E	MD	$18.44	1/1/2003

Information Specifications

Mr. Gonzalez requests an Employees by Insurance report and a Personalized Employee Enrollment report for each employee. Figures 2 and 3 show sketches of these reports. While you are free to work with the design of these reports, each report must provide the information shown in its sketch and have a professional appearance. The Employees by Insurance report associates employees with their chosen health insurance carriers. The Personalized Employee Enrollment report is a personalized report prepared for each employee. This report identifies the employee's current health benefits for a particular enrollment period.

The Employees by Insurance report sorts the information by insurance company and then sorts by employee name within the insurance company category. Each grouping is sorted in ascending order. For each employee, Mr. Gonzalez requests the employee's identification number, first and last name, and dependent code. Since this report requires data from multiple tables, you decide to create a select query, and then base the report on the select query. As part of the report's header, you include the report's title and current date.

Mr. Gonzalez wants each employee to receive a Personalized Employee Enrollment report. This report will be printed in January after the new rates take effect. Since this report requires data from multiple tables, you construct a select query, and then base the report on the select query. From the sketch in Figure 3, you notice that the header consists of a report title, current date, the employee's first and last names, department code, employee identification number, and monthly payroll deduction. You also notice that for each health benefit, the insurance company name, dependent code, and rate are printed. Since you use the ForceNewPage property to cause each employee's report to print on a new page, you do not need to design separate reports for each individual employee. (You may wish to use the system's online help to review the ForceNewPage property.)

Figure 2: Employees by Insurance Report

ABC **Employees by Insurance** ABC
(Current Date)

Insurance Company	Employee Identification Number	Last Name	First Name	Dependent Code
All American Life Care Company				
	00013	Enriquez	Antonio	C2
	00020	Timanus	Deona	S
Best Health Care				
	00010	Chee	Akiko	S2
	00011	Lou	Chia-Yi	E

Figure 3: Personalized Employee Enrollment Report

ABC **Personalized Employee Enrollment** ABC
(Current Date)

Prepared for: Antonio Enriquez **Department Code:** 01
Employee Identification No: 00013 **Monthly Payroll Deduction:** $284.45

Insurance Company	Dependent Code	Rate
Best Health Care	C2	$3.66
Midwest Dental	C2	$41.63
Perfect Vision	C2	$239.16

Mr. Gonzalez needs answers to the following questions. Build queries to help Mr. Gonzalez answer these questions. If you choose, you may generate reports based on these queries.

1. How many ABC employees are currently signed with an HMO? PPO?

2. How many ABC employees carry medical insurance for two or more children, but do not cover a spouse?

3. If vision insurance for an employee's dependents increases, how many employees are impacted?

4. Mr. Gonzalez wants a count of employees by insurance company. He wants the insurance company name, a description of the insurance company, and the count displayed.

5. Mr. Gonzalez wants a count of dependent code by insurance company. He wants the insurance company name, the dependent code name, and the dependent code count displayed.

Implementation Concerns

To make the changes specified in the case scenario, you will design and populate Employee and Select tables, create an Employee Insurance Enrollment form, establish relationships between tables, prepare an Employees by Insurance report, and prepare a Personalized Employee Benefits report for each employee. When building the Select table, use the Lookup Wizard to specify a list of values for the EID, DepCode, and InsCode fields.

You will define several relationships, in addition to the three relationships described in the Storage Specification section. For each relationship that you define, you should enforce referential integrity.

Although several ways exist for creating the Employee Insurance Enrollment form, you should consider using the Form Wizard. Once you have created the main form and subform, you can then edit each form. For additional information on subforms, use your system's online help feature.

While the Employees by Insurance report's design is straightforward, the Personalized Employee Enrollment report requires extra care. You should first build a query to retrieve the necessary data for the report, and then base the report on this query. In order to prepare this report according to Mr. Gonzalez's specifications, you will use the ForceNewPage property. Use your system's online help feature to learn more about this property.

Test Your Design

After creating the form, tables, relationships, queries, and reports, you should test your database design. Perform the following transactions:

1. The following employees are requesting changes to their health plans:
   - Mr. Ying Fang (00025) adds dental and vision insurance for his wife and two children.
   - Mrs. Donatica Angelo (00016) adds her spouse to her current coverage. He will be covered with Best Health Care and Perfect Vision.
   - Dr. Gayle Yates adds dental coverage for her spouse and five children. She does not recall her employee identification number.

2. ABC hired two new employees. Please enter the following information into the database.

Employee Name: Barbara Michaels   **Department:** 04
Employee Address: 1944 Calvin Boulevard   **Office Extension:** 4822
          Dallas, TX 75261

EID: XXXXX

Dependent Code	Insurance Code	Rate	Effective Date
S	AALC	XXX	3/15/2003
S	PV	XXX	3/15/2003
E	AALC	XXX	3/15/2003
E	PV	XXX	3/15/2003

Employee Name: Fredrico Behar   **Department:** 02
Employee Address: 2204 Pigeon Nest   **Office Extension:** 2797
          Garland, TX 75040

EID: XXXX

Dependent Code	Insurance Code	Rate	Effective Date
S1	AALC	XXX	5/1/2003
S1	PV	XXX	5/1/2003
S1	MD	XXX	5/1/2003
E	AALC	XXX	5/1/2003
E	PV	XXX	5/1/2003
E	MD	XXX	5/1/2003

3. Use the new rates in Table 1, and update the Rate table. You may wish to build a Rate form to help with data entry.

4. Which employees are impacted by an increase in their dental insurance? List the employee's first and last names.

CASE DELIVERABLES

In order to satisfactorily complete this case, you should build the database and then prepare both written and oral presentations. Unless otherwise specified, submit the following deliverables to your professor. Also, unless otherwise specified, perform these steps after you have tested your design.

1. A written report discussing any assumptions you have made about the case and the key elements of the case. Additionally, what features did you add to make the database more functional? User friendly? (Please note that these assumptions cannot violate any of the requirements specified above and must be approved by your professor.)

2. A printout of each form.

3. A printout of each report.

4. An electronic, working copy of your database that meets the criteria mentioned in the case scenario and specifications sections.

5. Results for each query. (A memo to your instructor discussing these results should also be provided.)

6. As mentioned above, you should prepare an oral presentation. (Your instructor will establish the time allocated to your presentation.) You should use a presentation package and discuss the key features of your database. Also, discuss how this database is beneficial for Mr. Gonzalez. What additional information from the database might Mr. Gonzalez find useful?

CASE 16

Wright Brothers' Airport Shuttle Service

Database Case　　　　**Difficulty Rating:** ★★★★

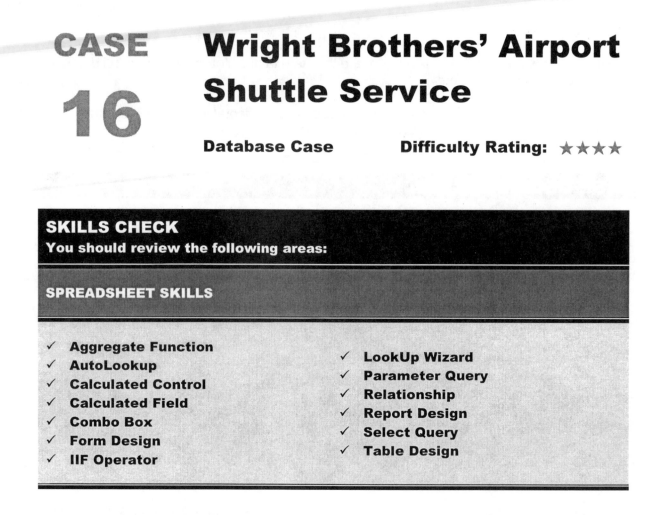

SKILLS CHECK
You should review the following areas:

SPREADSHEET SKILLS

- ✓ Aggregate Function
- ✓ AutoLookup
- ✓ Calculated Control
- ✓ Calculated Field
- ✓ Combo Box
- ✓ Form Design
- ✓ IIF Operator

- ✓ LookUp Wizard
- ✓ Parameter Query
- ✓ Relationship
- ✓ Report Design
- ✓ Select Query
- ✓ Table Design

CASE BACKGROUND

The Wright Brothers' Airport Shuttle Service provides economical off-airport parking and an airport shuttle service for its customers. Basil and Sage Wright, recognizing the advantage of offering these services to their customers, opened their off-airport parking and shuttle service two months ago. Since that time, they have watched demand for their business steadily increase. Basil, overwhelmed with paperwork, began developing a simple reservation database. The intent of the database is to track current parking space reservations. As of today, Basil has been unable to complete the database and has requested your help.

CASE SCENARIO

As a frequent traveler, Basil Wright recognizes the need for economical, off-airport parking. When an opportunity presented itself last year, Basil and his brother, Sage, purchased ten acres of land near the International Airport. The brothers have since converted a portion of their newly acquired land into a parking facility and provide a shuttle service for travelers. While Sage is responsible for shuttling travelers to and from the airport, Basil manages the business's daily paperwork activities.

Wright Brothers' Airport Shuttle Service offers valet parking, providing 200 covered valet parking spaces and 250 uncovered valet parking spaces. Covered parking is $7.00 per day, and uncovered parking is $6.00 per day.

When a customer arrives, he turns his car over to a parking attendant. The customer then walks into the office, provides necessary information to another attendant, requests covered or uncovered parking, receives a claim ticket, and then boards an airport shuttle. When a vehicle is checked in, the attendant uses a list of available parking spaces to determine where the car is to be parked. The vehicle is assigned a parking location, and a claim tag is hung from the vehicle's rearview mirror. When the valet parking customer returns, he calls the shuttle service, provides his claim ticket number, and then catches the next available shuttle to the parking facility. When he arrives at the parking facility, the parking attendant locates the customer's record by ticket number. The customer then pays his parking fees, picks up his car and leaves.

Basil began building a database for the parking and shuttle service last month. However, the parking facility's popularity keeps Basil very busy with its daily operations, so he has been unable to complete the database. Since you are Basil's good friend, you volunteer to continue working with the database. Initially, you will modify the database to track the company's current parking reservations.

Basil gives you a current reservation list and a copy of the incomplete database. After examining these items, you notice that the reservation list was created using a current word processing application and that the list contains basic, current reservation information. Since the reservation list is in an electronic format, you can copy and paste the list's contents into the Parking table, once the table is created.

The current database contains several tables, including Airline, Car, Model, and Rate tables. These tables are populated with data. These tables require very little, if any, modifications. However, you realize that a Parking table is necessary, as well as a Parking Reservation form, Daily Check-In and Tentative Check-Out reports, a relationship between the Car and Model tables, and several queries. Basil stresses that the database should be simple in its design. He also mentions that he does not need to keep information about his past customers, previously parked vehicles, or past reservations.

Storage Specifications

As mentioned previously, Basil began working on the parking facility's database last month. However, his busy schedule prohibits him from completing the database. He gives you the incomplete database and requests that you continue working on its development. Basil has already designed and populated the Airline, Car, Model, and Rate tables. You must now design and populate the Parking table.

Table 1 shows the Parking table's structure. As mentioned above, the data to populate this table is stored in an electronic file. Once you have designed the table, you can copy and paste the data into the appropriate fields.

Since the ticket number serves as the primary key, the attendant will enter a unique number for each ticket. You can assume that the ticket number is obtained from a preprinted claim ticket. To facilitate data entry, the Car Make, Car Model, Airline Abbreviation, and Rate Code values are obtained from a list of values. During table design, use the LookUp Wizard to create a list of values for each of these fields. Since Basil does not wish to keep historical information on his customers, information about customers who have claimed their vehicles will be deleted from the database. However, you are not required to develop a delete query for this exercise.

A relationship between the Car and Model tables is required. You should look for a common column between the two tables for which you are establishing a relationship. For instance, the Car and Model tables both have a MakeID column. You can use this field to establish a relationship between the two tables. Keep in mind that the columns are not required to have the same name, although in this instance they do.

Table 1: Parking Table Structure

Field Name	Data Type	Field Description	Field Size	Comments
Ticket Number	Number	Stores the claim ticket number. This number is unique.	Long Integer	Serves as primary key
Customer Last Name	Text	Stores the customer's last name.	50	Is required
Customer First Name	Text	Stores the customer's first name.	50	Is required
Check-In Date	Date/Time	Stores the date the vehicle is checked in.	Short Date	Is required
Check-Out Date	Date/Time	Stores the actual date the vehicle is picked up. Can differ from tentative return date.	Short Date	
Tag Number	Text	Stores the vehicle's tag number.	10	Is required
Tag State	Text	Identifies the state where the car is registered.	2	Use a default value of "OK"
Parking Location	Text	Identifies where the vehicle is parked.	5	Is required
MakeID	Number	Identifies the vehicle's make.	Long Integer	Is required
ModelID	Number	Identifies the vehicle's model.	Long Integer	
Tentative Return Date	Date/Time	Is the expected return date.	Short Date	

AAB	Text	Is the two-character airline code.	3	
Rate Code	Text	Identifies the designated rate code for the vehicle.	3	Is required
Comments	Memo	Used by the parking attendant to enter additional comments about the vehicle.		

Input Specifications

Figure 1 provides a sketch of the Parking Reservation form you will build. While you are free to modify the form's design, the form must have a professional appearance and capture the data shown in Figure 1.

As the parking attendant completes the form, you would like him to select a rate code and then have the Rate and Description fields automatically filled in. To accomplish this, you construct an AutoLookup query that uses data from both the Parking and Rate tables. When constructing this query, add all the fields from the Parking table. From the Rate table, add the Rate and Description fields.

Since you used the LookUp Wizard to create the Airline, Car Make, Car Model, and Rate Code fields in the Parking table, you realize that dropdown lists for these fields automatically appear on the Parking Reservation form. Using dropdown lists for these fields facilitates data entry, and you like this idea.

Current Charges is a calculated field. To calculate the customer's current charges, you multiply the difference between the Check-Out Date and the Check-In Date by Rate. However, after further analysis, you realize that this formula must also check to see if the customer has left and arrived on the same day. If a customer leaves and returns later on the same day, the difference between the Check-Out Date and the Check-In Date is zero. However, the customer should still be charged for one day of parking. You decide to modify your formula to check for this situation. You can use an immediate IF function to check for this condition. (If you are unfamiliar with the immediate IF function, please refer to the database tutorial or the system's online help for hints on how to use this function.)

Figure 1: Parking Reservation Form

Wright Brothers' Airport Shuttle Service

Parking Reservation Form

Ticket No: Check-In Date:
Customer Last Name: Tentative Return Date:
Customer First Name: Check-Out Date:
Airline:

Car Make: Covered Parking:
Car Model: Parking Location:
Tag:
Tag State:

                                                  Rate Code: Rate Description:
                                                  Rate:
                                                  Current Charges:

Comments:

Information Specifications

At the end of each day, Basil prepares two reports, a Daily Check-In Report and a Tentative Check-Out Report. The Daily Check-In Report lists each vehicle that was checked in that day. The Tentative Check-Out Report identifies vehicles scheduled for pickup the next day. Figures 2 and 3 provide sketches of these reports. While you are free to work with the design of these reports, each report must provide the information shown in its sketch and have a professional appearance.

As mentioned above, the Daily Check-In Report identifies vehicles that have been dropped off that day. You decide to base this report on a parameter query. By using a parameter query, the end user is asked to supply a date. The Daily Check-In Report also specifies how many parking spaces were required for each type of valet parking. A grand total is provided at the end of the report. To enhance readability, the report contents are sorted by the rate description and then by parking location within the rate description category. As part of the report's header, you should include a report title, the current date and a picture. You should locate an appropriate picture to include.

Figure 2: Daily Check-In Report

Wright Brothers' Airport Shuttle Service
Daily Check-In Report
(Current Date)

Covered/ Uncovered	Parking Location	Customer Last Name	Customer First Name	Ticket Number	Tag Number	Car Make	Car Model	Tentative Check-Out Date
Covered	C1	Bennett	Brooke	144	B7987	Mitsubishi	Montero	1/5/2003
	C3	Lansing	Larry	146	D4756	Lexus	ES250	1/7/2003
				Category Subtotal:				
Uncovered	U5	Farmer	David	145	IMOK4	Ford	Expo	1/4/2003
	U7	Yu	Samantha	148	IM47	Mazda	Miata	1/15/2003
				Category Subtotal:				
				Total Vehicles Checked In:				

At the end of each day, Mr. Wright prints a Tentative Check-Out Report. This report identifies the vehicles tentatively scheduled for pickup the next day. Mr. Wright wants this report sorted by parking location. He also wants to know how many vehicles are tentatively scheduled for pick up. Since the report is printed for a particular day, you will construct a parameter query. The parameter query requests the user to provide a specific date, and then a report is generated based on this date. This parameter query is similar to the one you constructed above. Figure 3 shows a sketch for the Tentative Check-Out Report.

Figure 3: Tentative Check-Out Report

Wright Brothers' Airport Shuttle Service

Tentative Check-Out Report
(Current Date)

Parking Location	Customer Last Name	Customer First Name	Ticket Number	Tag Number	Car Make	Car Model
C1	Adams	Audrey	144	B7987	Mitsubishi	Expo
C3	Lansing	Larry	146	D4756	Lexus	ES250
U5	Farmer	David	145	IMOK4	Ford	Expo
U7	Yu	Samantha	148	IM47	Mazda	Miata

Total Vehicles Scheduled for Pick Up:

Basil needs answers for the following questions. Build queries to help Basil answer these questions. If you choose, you may generate reports based on these queries. Also, base your answers on the data that are currently in the database. (Do not worry about whether a customer's record should have been deleted.)

1. What is the average length of stay for vehicles? What are the average earnings?

2. How many cars are utilizing covered parking? Uncovered?

3. How many cars were checked in today? Checked out? (Use 12/31/2003 as the current date.)

4. Which airline is used most frequently?

5. What percentage of covered valet parking spaces is used? What percentage of uncovered valet parking spaces is used? (Consider generating a report to answer this question.)

Implementation Concerns

In order to build the portion of the database described in the case scenario, you will build a table, a form, two reports, and several queries, including select, parameter, and AutoLookup queries. Several of the queries require you to sort, specify criteria, create expressions, and use data from two or more tables. Keep in mind that the form and reports are based on queries, so you should construct your queries before building the form and reports.

In order to design the reports, you base the reports on queries, specify sort orders, and work with report headers, footers, and page headers. To enhance the appearance of the form and reports, you should locate a picture to insert in the form or report header. The form and reports require calculated controls.

You will establish a relationship between the Car and Model tables. You should establish this relationship before designing your queries.

Test Your Design

After creating the table, form, queries, and reports, you should test your database design. Perform the following transactions.

1. The following customers have dropped off their cars. Enter this information into the database. You do not need to enter data into the Check-Out Date and Comments fields, so these fields are not shown in the following table.

Ticket Number	Customer Last Name	Customer First Name	Car Make ID	Car Model	Tag No	Tag State	Parking Location	Check-In Date	Tentative Return Date	AA B	Rate Code
400	Jester	Eleanor	Mitsubishi	Montero	E7T89	OK	U21	Enter Current Date	Scheduled to return 1 week from current date.	AA	1
401	Pellegrino	Allan	GMC	Envoy	YT090	OK	U22	Enter Current Date	Scheduled to return 2 weeks from current date.	WN	1
402	Ho	Chen	Cadillac	Escalade	KYRJT	TX	C14	Enter Current Date	Scheduled to return the next day.	HP	2
403	Yeh	Ling	Infiniti	G20	HI9864	TX	C19	Enter Current Date	Scheduled to return the next day.	PN	2
404	Polito	Ralph	Jeep	Grand Cherokee	KL76H	KS	C20	Enter Current Date	Scheduled to return 4 days from current date.	WN	2
405	Arnett	Benny	Buick	LeSabre	TR3345	KS	C21	Enter Current Date	Scheduled to return 1 week from current date.	AA	1

2. The following customers have claimed their cars.

Ticket Number	Customer Last Name	Customer First Name	Check-Out Date
9	Wodraska	Lester	January 3, 2003
10	Longfellow	Tabitha	January 3, 2003

3. Locate ticket number 11. What are the customer's current charges? Which airline did she use?

CASE DELIVERABLES

In order to satisfactorily complete this case, you should make the necessary modifications to the database and then prepare both written and oral presentations. Unless otherwise specified, submit the following deliverables to your professor. Also, unless otherwise specified, perform these steps after you have tested your design.

1. A written report discussing any assumptions you have made about the case and the key elements of the case. Additionally, what features did you add to make the database more functional? User friendly? (Please note that these assumptions cannot violate any of the requirements specified above and must be approved by your professor.)

2. A printout of each form.

3. A printout of each report. For the Tentative Check-Out Report, use January 3, 2003 as the current date. For the Check-In Report, use January 22, 2003 as the current date.

4. An electronic, working copy of your database that meets the criteria mentioned in the case scenario and specifications sections.

5. Results for each query. (A memo to your instructor discussing these results should also be provided.)

6. As mentioned above, you should prepare an oral presentation. (Your instructor will establish the time allocated to your presentation.) You should use a presentation package and discuss the key features of your database. Also, discuss how this database is beneficial for Basil. What modifications would make this database more beneficial for Basil?

CASE 17

Healthy Plant and Tree Nursery

Database Case　　　　**Difficulty Rating:** ★★★★★

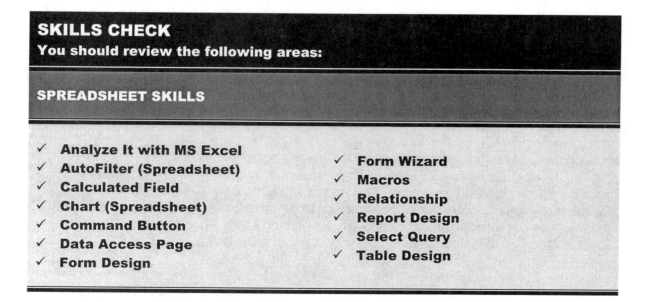

SKILLS CHECK

You should review the following areas:

SPREADSHEET SKILLS

- ✓ Analyze It with MS Excel
- ✓ AutoFilter (Spreadsheet)
- ✓ Calculated Field
- ✓ Chart (Spreadsheet)
- ✓ Command Button
- ✓ Data Access Page
- ✓ Form Design

- ✓ Form Wizard
- ✓ Macros
- ✓ Relationship
- ✓ Report Design
- ✓ Select Query
- ✓ Table Design

CASE BACKGROUND

Having operated in the sunny, southern Florida area for over 100 years, Healthy Plant and Tree Nursery is well known for raising quality plants and fruit trees, especially tropical varieties. The nursery's primary customers are local landscaping companies, home and garden stores, and individuals. All paperwork is manually performed, creating a headache for Juan Regaldo, the nursery's current owner. Mr. Regaldo also has problems keeping his store managers informed about the nursery's available inventory. In an effort to correct the mounting paperwork and communication problems, Mr. Regaldo hires you to build an inventory database for the nursery. After an initial meeting with Mr. Regaldo, you determine that a Product table, Current Inventory List page, Product form, Low-In-Stock report, and several select queries are necessary. Mr. Regaldo is especially interested in using the nursery's data to support decision-making activities. Since the nursery's data will soon be stored in electronic form, Mr. Regaldo requests the ability to analyze the data with Microsoft Excel.

CASE SCENARIO

Healthy Plant and Tree Nursery provides its customers with a wide selection of quality plants and trees, particularly tropical varieties. The nursery's inventory list includes many types of fruit trees, including mandarin orange, guava and mango. Trees are sold in containers, and the containers range in size from 7 to 25 gallons. The nursery also sells quality exotic plants, including Glorisa Superba, Yucca, and Medinilla. All nursery plants are sold in pots, ranging in size from 6 to 12-inch containers. Plant and tree prices are based on type and container size.

Currently, Healthy Plant and Tree Nursery has two stores and a nursery. Each location has Internet access and is capable of selling nursery items. The nursery location has several greenhouses where plants and trees are raised. When a plant or tree is ready for sale, it is moved to a special distribution greenhouse where all plants and trees ready for immediate distribution and sale are stored. Each evening, each store's inventory is checked, and a replenishment order is placed with the nursery. A replenishment order is filled from the distribution warehouse's current inventory and is usually delivered to the store the next day.

Occasionally, a customer requests a plant or tree that is not in the store's current inventory or makes a request for a large quantity of a particular plant or tree. If the store does not have a particular plant or tree in stock or does not have enough of the item in stock, the store manager calls the distribution greenhouse to determine if the plant or tree is available, when it can be delivered to the store and the quantity on hand. If the item is available, the product is reserved for the customer. Delivery is usually made the next day.

In the future, Mr. Regaldo wants store managers to access the nursery's current available inventory via the Internet, so that phone calls to the nursery are no longer necessary for small orders. If more than 50 units of any one item are required from the nursery's distribution warehouse, the store manager checks the Current Inventory List page and then calls Mr. Regaldo to place the units on reserve. Any order for less than 50 units of a particular item no longer requires a phone call to the nursery. Although Mr. Regaldo wants store managers to have access to inventory data, he does not want his store managers updating the nursery's inventory data. Mr. Regaldo feels these changes will improve the efficiency and performance of the nursery's operations. After reflecting on these requirements, you decide that a data access page easily satisfies these specifications.

Besides fielding phone calls from store managers, one of the most time-consuming activities for Mr. Regaldo is keeping the nursery's inventory records up-to-date. Mr. Regaldo requests the ability to identify which plants and trees in the distribution greenhouse are currently low in stock. He uses this information to restock the distribution greenhouse from the nursery's other greenhouses. A Low-In-Stock report satisfies this information request.

In addition to easing the data maintenance burden, Mr. Regaldo wants the capability to analyze the nursery's data with Microsoft Excel. In particular, Mr. Regaldo wants to determine his top selling items, gross margins, and inventory costs. He also wants the ability to prepare charts for presentations and analysis. This information will help him develop better marketing, pricing, and inventory stocking strategies. Mr. Regaldo asks you if it is possible to export the inventory data to a spreadsheet application, such as Microsoft Excel, for further analysis. Although several methods for moving data from a database to a spreadsheet exist, you recommend using the Analyze It with MS Excel feature. You explain to Mr. Regaldo that once the data are moved to Microsoft Excel, he can use Microsoft Excel to further support his decision-making needs.

Initially, Mr. Regaldo needs an inventory database to track the plants and trees currently housed in the distribution greenhouse. Later, he will include plants and trees from the nursery's other greenhouses in the inventory database. In order to build this database, you will design and populate a Product table; design a Product form, a Current Inventory List data access page, and a Low-In-Stock report; and create several select queries.

Storage Specifications

After reviewing Mr. Regaldo's information requirements, you decide the Nursery database requires a Product table. The Product table stores important inventory data about the plants and trees available for immediate sale and distribution. For each product, its product number, name, category, product cost, selling price, container size, and Quantity on Hand are stored. Table 1 shows the Product table's structure (Your instructor will provide you with the data necessary to populate the Product table.) Since the product number is unique for each product record, you decide this field should serve as the primary key. The category field indicates whether the item is a plant or tree. Since plants and trees are available in a variety of sizes, the container size field indicates the size of the pot or container. If the nursery item is a tree, its container size is measured in gallons. However, if the nursery item is a plant, its pot size is measured in inches.

Table 1: Product Table Structure

Field Name	Data Type	Field Description	Field Size	Comments
PNo	Long Integer	Contains the Product number. Serves as the primary key.	4	Is required.
PName	Text	Contains the name of the product.	25	Is required.
PCategory	Text	Is a two-digit code, indicating the type of product. Currently is either a tropical plant or fruit tree. All characters should display in uppercase.	2	Is required.
ProductCost	Currency	Shows the product's cost.	8	Is required.
SellingPrice	Currency	Indicates the retail price of the product.	8	Is required.
ContainerSize	Long Integer	Identifies the container size of the product.	4	Is required.
QOH	Long Integer	Identifies the quantity on hand of a particular product that is ready for distribution.	4	Is required.

Input Specifications

In order to maintain the nursery's inventory, a Product form is necessary. Figure 1 shows a tentative sketch for this form. As you examine the sketch, you realize that the form's header includes the nursery's name, the form's name, and graphics. For the graphics, you decide to locate a suitable picture of a plant or tree. The form's body contains all the fields from the Product table, so you use the Form Wizard to quickly build an initial Product form. Once the tentative Product form is created, you edit the form in Design view, providing the form with a more professional appearance.

During a recent conversation with Mr. Regaldo, he mentioned the need to simplify record navigation and operations. To satisfy this requirement, you decide the Product form should include Add, Find, Save, and Print buttons. Since the Command Button Wizard simplifies the inclusion of these buttons on the Product form, you use the Command Button Wizard to place these buttons on the form.

Figure 1: Product Form

	Healthy Plant and Tree Nursery	
	Product	

Product No: Container Size:
Product Name: QOH:
Product Category:

Product Cost:
Selling Cost:

| Add | Find | Save | Print |

Information Specifications

After studying your notes from a meeting with Mr. Regaldo, you decide that a Low-In-Stock report and a Current Inventory List page are necessary. The Low-In-Stock report identifies which of the distribution warehouse's plants and trees have less than 75 units on hand. Figure 2 provides a tentative sketch of the Low-In-Stock report. Mr. Regaldo wants the nursery's name, report title, current date, and graphics displayed in the report header. The report body lists the product's category, name, product number, container size, and quantity on hand. Mr. Regaldo wants the nursery items grouped in ascending order by category and then sorted in ascending order by product name. Although not shown in the sketch, Mr. Regaldo wants the page number printed in the report's page footer.

Mr. Regaldo wants store managers to have read-only access to the distribution warehouse's current inventory via the Internet. Since a data access page is a Web page that links to a Microsoft Access database, a store manager can easily view current inventory listings by using a browser, such as Internet Explorer 5.0 or higher. Also a data access page can provide read-only privileges, thus restricting a manager's ability to update inventory data. You use the Page Wizard to create an initial data access page, and then edit the page in Design view. Since Mr. Regaldo wants the Current Inventory List page to have a tropical appearance, you format the page using a Citrus Punch theme. Figure 3 shows a tentative sketch of the data access page.

Figure 2: Low-In-Stock Report

Healthy Plant and Tree Nursery
Low-In-Stock
(Current Date)

Category Name	Product Name	Product Number	Container Size	Quantity on Hand
FT	Allspice	30	10	75
	Allspice	5	15	50
	.			
	.			
	.			
TP	Glorisa Superba	22	6	15
	.			
	.			
	.			

Figure 3: Current Inventory List Page

Healthy Plant and Tree Nursery
Current Inventory List

Category Name	Product Name	Product Number	Container Size	Quantity On Hand	Selling Price
FT	Allspice	5	15	50	$69.48
FT	Allspice	30	10	75	$45.07
			.		
			.		
TP	Bonsai	6	24	159	$16.75
TP	Calathea	6	20	199	$12.75
			.		
			.		
			.		

Since Mr. Regaldo is familiar with spreadsheet applications, he asks if it is possible to export data from a database to a spreadsheet. He wants to use the spreadsheet's AutoFilter command to analyze the nursery's data. Specifically, Mr. Regaldo wants to export the product's number, name, category, cost, selling price, container size, and quantity on hand to Microsoft Excel. In addition, he wants the gross margin and total inventory cost for each product included in the worksheet. Since gross margin and total inventory cost are calculated fields, these data are not stored in the database. Although several methods for obtaining the gross margin and total inventory cost are available, you construct a select query that uses calculated fields to determine these values. Once the select query is constructed, you use the Analyze It with MS Excel tool to copy the dynaset to a worksheet. Once the dynaset is copied to the worksheet, Mr. Regaldo can analyze the data using any of Microsoft Excel's features.

Mr. Regaldo needs answers to the following questions. Use Excel's AutoFilter feature to answer these questions.

1. Which products have less than 20 units on hand?

2. What is the total cost of inventory? (You may find Microsoft Excel's Sum Function beneficial.)

3. Which products have the highest gross margin? (Show the top ten.)

4. Which products have the lowest gross margin? (Show the lowest five.)

5. For which products does the nursery have more than 300 units on hand?

Implementation Concerns

To build the database according to Mr. Regaldo's specifications, you will design and populate a Product table; design a Product form, Current Inventory List page, and Low-In-Stock report; construct select queries; and analyze data using Microsoft Excel. While you are free to work with the form, report, and data access page designs, these objects must have a professional, consistent appearance and utilize a tropical or citrus theme.

Consider using the available wizards to create the initial form, data access page and report. These objects can then be easily edited in Design view. The Page Wizard simplifies the creation of the Current Inventory List page. Once the data access page is created, you can edit the Inventory List page in Design view.

Although several methods for exporting data from a database to a spreadsheet application for further analysis exist, the Analyze It with MS Excel feature is a nice, easy tool to use. Before exporting the inventory data to Microsoft Excel, consider constructing a select query. The select query can retrieve the necessary data from the Product table and calculate the gross margin and inventory cost for each product. (You may wish to use your system's on-line help feature to review calculated fields.)

Test Your Design

After creating the table, form, data access page, report, and queries, you should test your database design. Perform the following steps.

1. Insert the following five new products.

PNo	PName	PCategory	PCost	SellingPrice	ContainerSize	QOH
41	Lemon	FT	$47.68	$62.95	10	150
42	Naval Orange	FT	$37.87	$50.25	10	100
43	Apricot	FT	$56.78	$74.95	10	270
44	Strelitzia	TP	$8.25	$16.95	10	500
45	Medinilla	TP	$8.25	$16.95	10	403

2. For each of the following nursery items, use the Product form to locate and then update its quantity on hand.

The nursery's distribution warehouse now has 175 15-gallon lime trees (PNo = 2) on hand.

The nursery's distribution warehouse now has 150 15-gallon cherry trees (PNo = 12) on hand.

The nursery's distribution warehouse now has 15 6-inch Glorisa Superba (PNo = 22), plants on hand.

3. Using the Product form, locate the Croton plant record (PNo = 16). Print this record.

4. Using Excel's AutoFilter feature, identify the ten nursery products that have the highest selling price. The products should be sorted in descending order by selling price.

5. Prepare a column chart showing the gross margin for each of the 15-gallon trees.

CASE DELIVERABLES

In order to satisfactorily complete this case, you should build the database and then prepare both written and oral presentations. Unless otherwise specified, submit the following deliverables to your professor. Also, unless otherwise specified, perform these steps after you have tested your design.

1. A written report discussing any assumptions you have made about the case and the key elements of the case. Additionally, what features did you add to make the database more functional? User friendly? (Please note that these assumptions cannot violate any of the requirements specified above and must be approved by your professor.)

2. A printout of each form.

3. A printout of each report, including the data access page.

4. An electronic, working copy of your database that meets the criteria mentioned in the case scenario and specifications sections.

5. An electronic working copy of your spreadsheet that meets the criteria mentioned in the case scenario.

6. Printouts showing the results for the questions asked in the Information Specification Section. (A memo to your instructor discussing these results should also be provided.)

7. Printouts showing the results for Test Your Design Section Steps 3, 4, and 5. (A memo to your instructor discussing these results should also be provided.)

8. As previously mentioned, you should prepare an oral presentation. (Your instructor will establish the time allocated to your presentation.) You should use a presentation package and discuss the key features of your database. Also, discuss how this database is beneficial for Mr. Regaldo. What additional data could be stored in the database?

9. What other types of decisions might Mr. Regaldo use Microsoft Excel to answer? You should identify at least two additional types of decisions. In addition to the chart mentioned above, identify at least one other chart that Mr. Regaldo might use.

CASE 18

Franklin University: Student Scholarship Management

Database Case   **Difficulty Rating:** ★★★★★

CASE BACKGROUND

Early each spring, Franklin University students apply for scholarships, tuition waivers, and various other awards for the next academic year by completing general scholarship applications. Students leave the completed general scholarship applications with their college dean's office. After the application deadline has passed, the applications are forwarded to the appropriate departments, based on student major. The departments review the general scholarship applications and make awards. While each department wants deserving students to receive the awards to which the students are entitled, the departments do not want to allocate money that cannot be used. Until recently, no central source could help the departments determine if a student already had most, if not all, of his college fees covered. One of the major tasks of the newly formed Franklin University Scholarship Office is to track all awards, scholarships, and tuition waivers that have been granted. Although the departments are still responsible for identifying award recipients, the departments will now work closely with the Franklin University Scholarship Office to avoid any overlap with awards. You are hired to develop a Scholarship database for the Franklin

University Scholarship Office and to assist with the award distributions. Development entails designing and populating an Award table; designing Award and Applicant forms; preparing Award Availability, In-State Tuition Waiver Eligibility, Applicant By Major, and Award Recipient List reports; creating Main, Form, Query, and Report switchboards; constructing several queries; and creating a macro.

CASE SCENARIO

Each spring semester, a Franklin University student interested in obtaining an award, tuition waiver, or scholarship completes a general scholarship application. The student then drops his completed application off at his college dean's office. From there, the dean's office forwards the application to the appropriate department for evaluation. Although this application process has merit, this decentralized approach to allocating awards to students has created numerous problems. The university often finds that a multiple-award winning student is unable to use all the money allocated to him. For instance, tuition waivers are only applicable to general enrollment fees and cannot be applied to other educational expenses, such as room, board, or technology fees. So, if a student receives multiple tuition waivers from various sources, these tuition waivers can only pay for the student's general enrollment fees. He cannot use the excess tuition waiver money to pay for any other educational expenses. The unused money is left in an account until the end of the semester or academic year, depending on how it was earmarked for distribution. Since this money is not reallocated in a timely fashion, other deserving students are unable to take advantage of the unused award money.

In an effort to better coordinate the award distribution process, the Franklin University Scholarship Office is now responsible for coordinating the award distribution activities. You are hired to assist Franklin University's Scholarship Director, Simona Xavier, in managing the award distributions.

Ms. Xavier explains that the new process works as follows. During March, an Awards Availability report, along with the general scholarship applications relevant to the particular college, are distributed to each college. The Awards Availability report reminds the college and departments about the awards available for each college and department and the amount allocated for each award. The departments then meet, evaluate applications, and make recommendations for awards. The departments submit Tentative Award Allocation reports to the Franklin University Scholarship Office. The Franklin University Scholarship Office staff enters the information from the Tentative Award Allocation reports into the Scholarship database and cross checks the award recipients to make sure that the recipients are only receiving awards that can be used. For instance, an applicant may receive a Merit Credit Scholarship and a tuition waiver from a department. Since each of these awards provides tuition assistance, one of these awards could be reallocated to another deserving student.

Ms. Xavier hands you a partially completed Scholarship database and asks you to finish building the database. After reviewing the database contents, you decide the database requires Award and Applicant forms; Main, Form, Query, and Report switchboards; Award Availability, In-State Tuition Waiver Eligibility, Applicant By Major, and Award Recipient List reports; several queries; and a macro. Ms. Xavier specifically asks that the Scholarship database be user friendly and provide "push of a button" access to the most frequently used forms, reports, and queries.

Storage Specifications

The current Scholarship database contains Applicant and Allocation tables. When a student submits a general scholarship application, data from this application are entered and stored in the Applicant table. As you study the Applicant table, you notice that this table has several fields, including fields for the student's basic contact information, current GPA, completed hours, expected hours for each semester, major, general comments, instate tuition, and expected graduation date. The completed hours indicate how many hours the student has on his transcript, and the expected hours gives an indication about how many hours, on average, the student expects to carry each semester. The InStateTuition field indicates whether or not the student pays instate tuition fees. A student identification number serves as the primary key for the Applicant table. The Allocation table stores information about the awards a student receives. This table uses a combination key, consisting of award identification number and student identification number fields.

As you examine the Scholarship database, you realize that an Award table is necessary. This table stores information about each available award, including an award identification number, name, maximum available amount per student, total available amount, a designation indicating whether the award is an internal or external award, a designation indicating if the award is a departmental award, and general guidelines for administering the award. While a department or college gives an internal award, an external foundation or organization provides an external award. Also, an award is associated with a particular department or is given to a student who meets certain criteria, regardless of the student's college or major. For instance, the MIS Faculty Merit Scholarship is an internal award and is given each year to an outstanding MIS student. In contrast, the Bob Horan Foundation Scholarship is an external award and is available to any qualifying student, regardless of his college or major. Table 1 shows the Award table's structure. (Your instructor will provide you with the data to populate this table.)

As you study your notes, you decide two relationships are necessary. First, a relationship is necessary between the Award and Allocation tables. Since the Award and Allocation tables each have an AwardNo field, you use the AwardNo field to establish a relationship between the two tables. Second, a relationship between the Allocation and Applicant tables is necessary. Since the Allocation and Applicant tables have an SID field, you use the SID field to establish a relationship between these tables. You also enforce referential integrity for each relationship.

Table 1: Award Table Structure

Field Name	Data Type	Field Description	Field Size	Comments
AwardNo	Long Integer	Serves as primary key.	4	For each award, assign the next available number. Is required.
AwardName	Text	Specifies the name of the award.	50	Is required.
Internal?	Yes/No	Indicates whether the funding source is an organization outside the university. Mark "No" only if it is a company or foundation. Government sources are considered internal.	1	
Department?	Yes/No	Indicates whether the award or scholarship is specific to a particular department.	1	
CollegeAffiliation	Text	Indicates the college for which this award is targeted.	4	The field values should display in all caps.
MajorCode	Text	Indicates the major code for which the award is targeted.	4	
MaxStudentAmount	Currency	Indicates the maximum amount that can be given to a single student.	8	Is required.
TotalAvailable	Currency	Indicates the total amount allocated for this award.	8	Is required.
TuitionOnly	Yes/No	Designates whether this award can only be used for tuition and general fees.	1	
Guidelines	Memo	Provides the criteria for this award.		

Input Specifications

The Scholarship database requires Award and Applicant forms. The Award form enables end users to update information about existing awards and also add new awards. While the Award form updates data in the Award table, the Applicant form updates data in two tables: the Applicant and Allocation tables. The Applicant form captures details about the applicant and details about any awards the applicant receives. Since the Award form is the easier form to build, you decide to design it first and then work on the Applicant form.

Figure 1 shows a tentative sketch for the Award form. As Figure 1 indicates, the Award form includes all the fields from the Award table, so you use the Form Wizard to quickly create an initial Award form. Once the initial form is created, you edit the Award form in Design view. The Award form's header section includes the Franklin University Scholarship Office's name, the form name, and graphics. (You should locate an acceptable graphic to include in the form's header.)

Figure 1: Award

Franklin University Scholarship Office

Award

Award No:

Award Name:

Maximum Amount Per Student:

Total Amount Available:

Internal:

Department:

Tuition Only:

College Affiliation:

Major Code:

Guidelines:

The Applicant form captures information about each applicant and any awards he receives. Figure 2 provides a tentative sketch for this form. The form header includes the Franklin University Scholarship Office name, the form's name and graphics. The Applicant form includes all the fields from the underlying Applicant table and identifies, for each award, the award number, name, and award amount that a student received.

Since the award number, name, and award amount reference data stored in the Allocation table, a subform is necessary. (You may wish to use your system's online help feature to review subform design at this point.) Of special interest to Ms. Xavier is the ability to see, at a glance, the total dollar value of the awards a student received. You use a calculated field on the subform to sum the dollar amount of the received awards. You then reference the subform field on the main form. You use a calculated field on the main form and use the following expression to reference the subform's field. (Keep in mind that you need to modify the following expression to reflect the names you have given your main form, subform, and fields. Also, you may wish to use your system's online help feature to obtain additional information about calculated fields, expressions, and referencing fields.)

=[Forms!][Main Form Name]![Subform Name]![Field Name]

Figure 2: Applicant

Franklin University Scholarship Office

Applicant

Student Identification No: City: In-State:
Student First Name: State: Expected Hours:
Student Last Name: Zip: Completed Hours:
                                                  Expected Graduation Date:

Major:
GPA:

Comments:

Allocated Awards:

Award No.	Award Name	Award Amount

Total Allocation: $XXX.XX

Ms. Xavier requests easy access to the database's various forms, reports, and queries. She literally wants to "push a button or two" and view the requested object. Since a switchboard provides a standard interface, you decide to create four switchboards: Main, Form, Query, and Report. The Main switchboard page serves as a main menu, providing access to the other switchboard pages. The Form switchboard provides access to the database's forms, the Query switchboard provides access to the database's queries, and the Report switchboard provides access to the database's reports.

Figures 3 and 4 show tentative sketches for the Main and Form switchboards. (The Query and Report switchboards should use a similar format to the Main and Form switchboards.) On the Main switchboard, the last switchboard item, Exit to Franklin Database, enables the user to go to the database window. In order to perform this function, you create a macro and assign this macro to the Exit to Franklin Database button. (You may wish to use your system's online help feature to review macro and switchboard creation at this point.) Figure 4 provides a tentative sketch for the Form switchboard. As Figure 4 shows, the Form switchboard provides access to the forms in the database. You also place an option that enables the user to return to the Main switchboard. The Report and Query switchboards also include buttons that return the user to the Main switchboard.

Figure 3: Main Switchboard

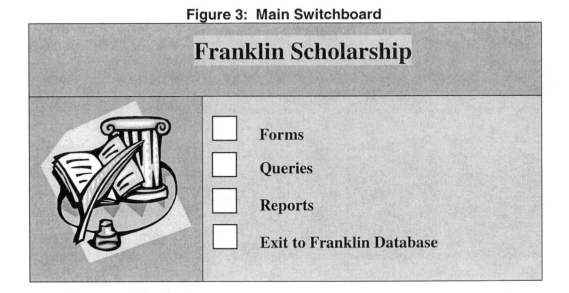

Figure 4: Form Switchboard

Information Specifications

Ms. Xavier requires Award Availability, In-State Tuition Waiver Eligibility, Applicant By Major, and Award Recipient List reports. Figure 5 provides a tentative sketch for the Award Availability report. This report identifies the available awards for the coming academic year. A designation of "UNIV" in the college affiliation or major code fields means that the award is not restricted to a particular college or department. Likewise, a designation of "CBA" means that the award is given to a particular college, but is not restricted to a particular department or major. The report header includes the scholarship office's name, the report's name, a current date, and graphics. The report information is sorted by college affiliation, then by major code and by award name within each major code category.

Figure 5: Award Availability

Franklin University Scholarship Office

Award Availability

(Current Date)

College Affiliation	Major Code	Award Name	Amount Per Student	Total Amount Available
CBA	411	Caedee Hannah Excellence Award	$3,500	$3,500
CBA	411	MIS Faculty Award	$800	$800
		.		
		.		
		.		
UNIV	UNIV	Merit Credit Award	$1,500	$20,000
		.		
		.		
		.		

The In-State Tuition Waiver Eligibility report, shown in Figure 6, identifies which students pay in-state tuition and are eligible for state tuition waivers. The report header includes the scholarship office's name, the report's name, the current date, and graphics. Ms. Xavier request that you locate suitable graphics for the report. As Figure 6 shows, the report body contains the student's last and first name, student identification number, major, expected hours, and expected graduation date. The information is sorted in ascending order by student last name. Although not shown in the sketch, Ms. Xavier requests that a page number be placed in the page footer.

Figure 6: In-State Tuition Waiver Eligibility

Franklin University Scholarship Office

In-State Tuition Waiver Eligibility

(Current Date)

Name	SID	Major	Expected Hours	Expected Graduate Date
Arenivar, Aaron	231717578	417	12	5/14/2003
Bernaldo, Delorise	652134881	411	12	5/14/2003
.				
.				
.				
Lowe, Ruby	218392004	416	12	7/31/2006
.				
.				
.				

Ms. Xavier periodically needs to view the applicants by major. She asks if it is possible to specify a major code and then generate a report. To satisfy this requirement, you build a parameter query and then base the Applicant By Major report on this query. Figure 7 shows a tentative sketch for this report. The report header includes the scholarship office's name and report name, specifies the major code, shows the current date, and includes graphics. The report body shows the first and last name, student identification number, GPA, completed hours, expected hours, and expected graduation date for each applicant. The report information is sorted in ascending order by last name.

Figure 7: Applicant By Major

Franklin University Scholarship Office

Applicant By Major

Major Code: 411

(Current Date)

Name	SID	GPA	Completed Hours	Expected Hours	Expected Graduation Date
Bernaldo, Delorise	652134881	3.64	94	12	5/14/2003
Chambers, James	660635664	3.12	99	12	5/14/2003
			.		
			.		
			.		
Noels, Frank	100496263	3.77	60	12	7/31/2005
			.		
			.		
			.		

The Award Recipient List identifies the applicants and the awards they received. This report is generated after all awards are given and is then distributed to the college deans and department chairpersons. Figure 8 shows a tentative sketch of the Award Recipient List. The Award Recipient List report header includes the scholarship office's name, the name of the report, a current date, and graphics. As Figure 8 illustrates, the report body alphabetically lists the students by last name, and then lists the awards each student received. For each student, the total dollar value of his awards is shown. Although not shown in Figure 8, a page number is included in the page footer.

Figure 8: Award Recipient List

Franklin University Scholarship Office

Award Recipient List

(Current Date)

Student Name	SID	Award Name	Award Amount
Dennington, Louise	012780183	Bob Horan Foundation Scholarship	$1,500.00
		MIS Department Tuition Waiver	$350.00
		Total Value:	**$1,850.00**
		.	
		.	
		.	
Ninemire, Guy	122388169	Marketing Department Tuition Waiver	$450.00
		Total Value:	**$450.00**

Ms. Xavier requires answers to the following questions. Build queries to help Ms. Xavier answer these questions. If you choose, you may generate reports based on these queries.

1. Which applicants are seniors? Provide the first and last names for these applicants. Do not show any other fields.

2. How many applicants have GPAs greater than 3.5? Show each applicant's first name, last name, and GPA. Do not show any other fields.

3. What is the average amount of award money that the applicants received?

4. What are the guidelines for the Bob Horan Foundation Scholarship award?

5. How much money is available for the CBA Outstanding Student award? What are the criteria for this award? Prepare a list of applicants that you feel meet the criteria for this award.

6. Which applicants did not receive an award? Why do you think the applicants did not receive an award?

7. Which applicants received more than one tuition waiver? Provide their names, the awards, and award amounts. Should any of the money be reallocated?

Implementation Concerns

The specifications presented in the case scenario require you to build and populate an Award table, create relationships among tables; design Award and Applicant forms; design Award Availability, In-State Tuition Waiver Eligibility, Applicant By Major, Award Recipient List reports; prepare Main, Form, Query, and Report switchboards; construct several queries; and create a macro.

The Form Wizard easily creates the Award form. Once created, the Award form can be modified in Design view. The Applicant form consists of both a main form and a subform. Although several methods exist for creating the Applicant form and its subform, one method is to use the Form Wizard. Once you have created the main form and subform, you can then edit each form. (For additional information on subforms, use your system's online help feature.) The Total Allocation field on the Applicant form is a calculated field. Consider including on your subform a field that sums the dollar amount for each award a student receives. Then reference this field on your main form. The Input Specification Section provides the expression that you can use to reference the subform field from your main form.

As part of this case, you are asked to create four switchboards. In essence, a switchboard is a menu. A switchboard presents the user with a standard interface or method for accessing database objects. Use the Main switchboard to branch to a Form switchboard, a Query switchboard and a Report switchboard.

You are asked to display the Main switchboard at startup. This is an easy feature to implement. To learn more about this feature, use the system's online help and request information about "displaying the switchboard on startup." Also, the last button on the Main switchboard page requires you to exit to the database window, not exit the application. To accomplish this task, you must create a macro and then assign the macro to the "Exit to Franklin Database" button.

You are free to work with the design of the forms, reports and switchboards. However, each object should have a professional, consistent format. Also, at a minimum, the Query switchboard should provide access to at least five queries.

Test Your Design

After creating the forms, tables, relationships, queries, reports, and macro, you should test your database design. Perform the following transactions:

145

1. The following students have applied for scholarships:

Student Identification No: 63548780
Student Last Name: Zeytounian
Student First Name: Ossie
Street Address: 101 Mockingbird Lane
City: Los Angeles
State: CA   **Zip:** 90016
In-State: Yes
Major: 411
Expected Hours: 15
Completed Hours: 93
GPA: 3.22
Expected Graduation Date: 5/14/2003

Student Identification No: 25972225
Student Last Name: Yu
Student First Name: Linda
Street Address: 2874 Pippin Street
City: Los Angeles
State: CA   **Zip:** 90017
In-State: No
Major: 417
Expected Hours: 18
Completed Hours: 88
GPA: 3.57
Expected Graduation Date: 12/14/2004

Student Identification No: 48484329
Student Last Name: Abernathy
Student First Name: Lamont
Street Address: 7878 Baylee Way
City: Los Angeles
State: CA   **Zip:** 90017
In-State: Yes
Major: 411
Expected Hours: 12
Completed Hours: 36
GPA: 3.77
Expected Graduation Date: 5/14/2006

Student Identification No: 58485529
Student Last Name: Beaumont
Student First Name: Joan
Street Address: 7584 Harrison Street
City: Los Angeles
State: CA   **Zip:** 90018
In-State: No
Major: 413
Expected Hours: 15
Completed Hours: 80
GPA: 3.98
Expected Graduation Date: 7/31/2004

2. The Franklin University Scholarship Office has been notified about two new awards. Enter the following information into the database:

Award Number: 15
Award Name: Friends of Education Award
Total Amount: $750
Maximum Per Student: $750
Internal: Yes
Departmental: No
Tuition Only: No
Guidelines: Is given to a senior with an outstanding GPA. The student must have at least a 3.75 GPA. Must be active on campus.

Award Number: 16
Award Name: Mary Lou Memorial Fund
Total Amount: $1,000
Maximum Per Student: $1,000
Internal: No
Departmental: Yes
Tuition Only: No
Guidelines: Is given to an MIS major. The student should demonstrate need.

3. Which scholarships have not been awarded? Prepare a report.

4. Ms. Xavier wants to know each applicant's rank and the awards the applicant received. Display the applicant's last and first name, rank, award name, and award amount. (Hint: Use the following table to determine the student's rank. Also, consider using the IIF function.)

Table 2: Student Classification

Rank	Hours Completed
Senior	90 or more
Junior	60 - 89
Sophomore	30 - 59
Freshman	0 - 29

CASE DELIVERABLES

In order to satisfactorily complete this case, you should build the database and then prepare both written and oral presentations. Unless otherwise specified, submit the following deliverables to your professor. Also, unless otherwise specified, perform these steps after you have tested your design.

1. A written report discussing any assumptions you have made about the case and the key elements of the case. Additionally, what features did you add to make the database more functional? User friendly? (Please note that these assumptions cannot violate any of the requirements specified above and must be approved by your professor.)

2. A printout of each form.

3. A printout of each report. (Where applicable, use a major code of 411.)

4. An electronic, working copy of your database that meets the criteria mentioned in the case scenario and specifications sections.

5. Results for each query. (A memo to your instructor discussing these results should also be provided.)

6. As mentioned above, you should prepare an oral presentation. (Your instructor will establish the time allocated to your presentation.) You should use a presentation package and discuss the key features of your database. Also, discuss how this database is beneficial for Ms. Xavier. What additional information from the database might Ms. Xavier find useful?

CASE 19

Mountain View Dental Clinic

Web Case   **Difficulty Rating:** ★★

CASE BACKGROUND

Dr. Joshi Michailoff owns a thriving, private dental practice in the northeastern United States. Dr. Michailoff and his staff provide a variety of dental services to both children and adults. Dr. Michailoff has noticed that many dental clinics have informative, useful Web pages for their patients. Since he is interested in attracting new patients and providing information for his current patients, he asks you to design a professional-looking Web page for his dental clinic.

CASE SCENARIO

The Mountain View Dental Clinic is a family-oriented dental practice, located in the northeastern United States. The dental clinic caters to both children and adults. Dr. Joshi Michailoff opened the clinic ten years ago, after graduating from the University of Texas Health Science Center, with a Doctor of Dental Surgery degree. Dr. Michailoff is a member of several organizations, including the American Dental Association, American Academy of Cosmetic Dentistry, Academy of General Dentistry, and American Association of Hospital Dentists. He recently was awarded the Fellowship in the Academy of General Dentistry, a very prestigious honor.

Dr. Michailoff has a wonderful support staff that includes Dianne Hamrick, Benita Jackson, Clyde McGill, and Corey Passey. Dianne is a dental assistant and has worked with Dr. Michailoff for the last 6 years. Benita is also a dental assistant and has worked at the clinic for the last year. Clyde is a dental hygienist and has worked at the clinic for 2 years, and Corey is the office manager and has worked at the clinic for the last 6 months.

The dental clinic provides a variety of services, including teeth cleaning, fluoride treatments, crowns and bridges, extractions, oral examinations, fillings, cosmetic bonding, porcelain veneers, teeth whitening, sealants, gum treatment, root canals, and partial and complete dentures. Payment for any of these services is expected at the time the service is provided. Patients may pay by major credit card, cash, check, or approved insurance.

The clinic's hours are Monday through Friday, from 9:00 a.m. to 5:00 p.m. Dr. Michailoff may be paged after hours for emergency care. Same day care is provided for most emergencies.

Dr. Michailoff asks you to design a Web page for his dental practice. He wants the Web page to promote his practice, provide basic information about the clinic, and attract new patients.

Design Specifications

Dr. Michailoff asks you to create an informative, professional-looking Web page. When his patients visit the Web page, Dr. Michailoff wants them to find an attractive, easily navigated page. Dr. Michailoff wants the Web page to serve as an information source for both current and future patients. At a minimum, he wants the Web page to provide basic information about the dental clinic, such as office hours, contact information, services, and staff. He wants the Web page's visitors to easily move around the site, and he wants the page to load quickly and contain links to other places of interest. He asks you to locate several of these sites.

Information Specifications

Before publishing the Web page, you want Dr. Michailoff to view the Web page. Dr. Michailoff has specifically said that he wants to view the following information on his clinic's Web page.

1. Dr. Michailoff wants to see the clinic's emergency care information.

2. Dr. Michailoff wants to see brief profiles for the clinic's staff. He feels this will help the patients feel more comfortable. (You should provide brief profiles for the staff.)

3. Dr. Michailoff wants to see a listing of the services provided by the clinic.

4. Dr. Michailoff wants the Web page to provide links to Web sites that contain useful information for dental patients. (You will need to supply this information.)

Implementation Concerns

The case scenario provides you with a broad background for the dental clinic. In several instances, you will need to make assumptions about the dental clinic in order to design an appropriate Web page. One helpful way to locate this information is to visit other dental clinic Web sites to see what information they display. However, keep in mind that you should not violate any existing copyrights.

While you are free to work with the design of the dental clinic's Web page, the Web page must have a consistent, professional appearance. Also, you should locate suitable graphics for the Web page. You instructor will provide you with additional requirements for the Web page.

Test Your Design

After creating the Web page, you should test your design. Perform the following steps.

1. Dr. Michailoff has recently hired a new dentist. Dr. Ashok Patmon recently graduated from a well-known dental school. Dr. Michailoff asks you to develop a short profile for Dr. Patmon and then add his profile to the dental clinic's Web page. (You will need to provide the necessary profile information.)

2. Often a patient's bill for his dental care can be substantial. As a way of alleviating the financial burden, Dr. Michailoff is instituting a new payment plan called the Dental Care Monthly Payment Plan. This plan provides established patients with a way to make monthly payments, rather than having to pay the entire fee at the time the services are rendered. Dr. Michailoff wants this information added to the clinic's Web page.

CASE DELIVERABLES

In order to satisfactorily complete this case, you should build the Web page and then prepare both written and oral presentations. Unless otherwise specified, submit the following deliverables to your professor. Also, unless otherwise specified, perform these steps after you have tested your design.

1. A written report discussing any assumptions you have made about the case and the key elements of the case. Additionally, what features did you add to make the Web page more functional? User friendly? (Please note that these assumptions cannot violate any of the requirements specified above and must be approved by your professor.)

2. A printout of the Web page. (If additional pages are created, you must submit these pages.)

3. An electronic, working copy of your Web page that meets the criteria mentioned in the case scenario and specifications sections.

4. As mentioned above, you should prepare an oral presentation. (Your instructor will establish the time allocated to your presentation.) You should use a presentation package and discuss the key features of your Web page. Also, discuss how the Web page is beneficial for Dr. Michailoff and his clinic. What additional information might Dr. Michailoff's patients find useful?

CASE
20

Family Veterinary Pet Care Clinic

Web Case   **Difficulty Rating:** ★★

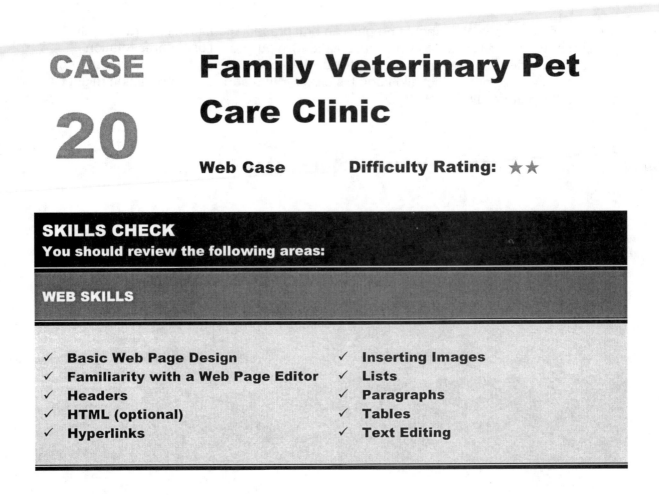

CASE BACKGROUND

Dr. Paul Tao owns a small veterinary practice in the southwest United States. Dr. Tao and his staff provide a variety of quality services and products to caring pet owners. Dr. Tao has noticed that several other veterinary clinics in the area have Web pages. In an effort to keep up with the times, he asks you to design a professional-looking Web page for his clinic.

CASE SCENARIO

The Family Veterinary Pet Care Clinic is a small veterinary clinic located in the southwest United States, specializing in the care of small animals. Dr. Paul Tao opened the clinic almost 20 years ago, after graduating with a doctor of veterinary medicine degree in 1983. Dr. Tao has received numerous national and community awards, including the prestigious AVMA Animal Welfare Award. Dr. Tao is a member of the American Veterinary Medical Association and American Animal Hospital Association and holds veterinary licenses in Texas, New Mexico, Arizona, and Oklahoma.

The veterinary clinic is well staffed by caring professionals, including a veterinary technician, office manager, and several veterinary assistants. Isla Meiring is a veterinary technician and has worked at the clinic for almost 15 years. Mario Schwermer is the office manager and has worked at the clinic for 5 years; Valerie Widick, Harriett Lafollette, Brian Hallett, and Bill McKee are veterinary assistants at the clinic. Valerie has worked at the clinic for 10 years, Harriett has worked at the clinic for two years, Brian has worked at the clinic for 6 months, and Bill was hired last week. Gary Dromgoole and Jules Dubois are groomers and have worked at the clinic since it opened in the 1980s.

The Family Veterinary Pet Care Clinic offers a wide range of services, including routine exams, surgery, radiology, pharmacy, orthopedic, dental, vaccinations, grooming, boarding, intensive care, home visitations, delivery of medications and supplies, and emergency care. As a full care pet clinic, the veterinary clinic offers a variety of products, including such items as accessories, dental, diet, cleaning products, medications, skin care, and dietary supplements. Payment for services and supplies is due when the services are rendered or the supplies are purchased. Clients may pay by cash, check, or major credit card. When using a credit card, all purchases must be over $25.00.

The clinic's hours are Monday through Friday, from 8:00 a.m. to 6:00 p.m., and on Saturday, from 8:00 a.m. to 12:00 p.m. Dr. Tao may be paged after hours for emergency care. Clients are encouraged to call for appointments; however, walk-ins are accepted.

During a recent conversation with Dr. Tao, he asked you to build a Web page for the clinic. He wants the Web page to promote his clinic, as well as provide basic information about the clinic.

Design Specifications

Dr. Tao asks you to create an informative, professional-looking Web page. When his clients visit the Web page, Dr. Tao wants them to find an attractive, easily navigated page. Dr. Tao wants the Web page to target individuals in the community who have small animals. At a minimum, he wants the Web page to provide basic information about the clinic, such as office hours, services, staff, and products. He wants the Web page's visitors to easily move around the site, and he wants the page to load quickly and contain links to other places of interest. He asks you to locate several of these sites.

Information Specifications

Before publishing the Web page, you want Dr. Tao to view the Web page. Dr. Tao has specifically said that he wants to view the following information on his clinic's Web page.

1. Dr. Tao wants to see the clinic's hours, as well as its emergency care information.

2. Dr. Tao wants to see brief profiles for the clinic's staff. He feels this will help the clients feel more comfortable.

3. Dr. Tao wants to see the clinic's policy on boarding animals. (You will need to supply this information.)

4. Dr. Tao wants to see a listing of his products organized by category, along with pricing information. (You will need to supply this information.)

5. Dr. Tao wants the Web page to provide links to Web sites that contain useful information for pet owners. (You will need to supply this information.)

Implementation Concerns

The case scenario provides you with a broad background for the veterinary clinic. In several instances, you will need to make assumptions about the clinic in order to design an appropriate Web page. One helpful way to locate this information is to visit other veterinary Web sites to see what information they display. However, keep in mind that you should not violate any existing copyrights.

While you are free to work with the design of the clinic's Web page, the Web page must have a consistent, professional appearance. Also, you should locate suitable graphics for the Web page. You instructor will provide you with additional requirements for the Web page.

Test Your Design

After creating the Web page, you should test your design. Perform the following steps.

1. Dr. Tao recently hired a new veterinarian. Dr. Lawanda Fontaine recently graduated from a well-known veterinary school. Dr. Tao asks you to develop a short profile for her and then add her profile to the clinic's Web page. (You will need to provide the necessary profile information.)

2. Often a client's bill for his pet can be substantial. As a way of alleviating the financial burden, Dr. Tao is instituting a new payment plan called the *Pet Care Extended Payment Plan*. This plan provides established clients with a way to make monthly payments, rather than having to pay the entire fee at the time the services are rendered. Dr. Tao wants this information added to the clinic's Web page.

CASE DELIVERABLES

In order to satisfactorily complete this case, you should build the Web page and then prepare both written and oral presentations. Unless otherwise specified, submit the following deliverables to your professor. Also, unless otherwise specified, perform these steps after you have tested your design.

1. A written report discussing any assumptions you have made about the case and the key elements of the case. Additionally, what features did you add to make the Web page more functional? User friendly? (Please note that these assumptions cannot violate any of the requirements specified above and must be approved by your professor.)

2. A printout of the Web page. (If additional pages are created, you must submit these pages.)

3. An electronic, working copy of your Web page that meets the criteria mentioned in the case scenario and specifications sections.

4. As mentioned above, you should prepare an oral presentation. (Your instructor will establish the time allocated to your presentation.) You should use a presentation package and discuss the key features of your Web page. Also, discuss how the Web page is beneficial for Dr. Tao and his clinic. What additional information might Dr. Tao's clients find useful?